CHILI

WITHDRAWN

D1473974

Other Cookbooks by A. D. Livingston

Jerky
Sausage
Cold-Smoking & Salt-Curing Meat, Fish, & Game
Cast-Iron Cooking
The Curmudgeon's Book of Skillet Cooking
Complete Fish & Game Cookbook
The Freshwater Fish Cookbook
Venison Cookbook
The Whole Grain Cookbook

CHILI

RECIPES FOR A BODACIOUS BOWL OF RED

A. D. LIVINGSTON

LYONS PRESS
Guilford, Connecticut

An imprint of Globe Pequot Press

Lyons Press is an imprint of Globe Pequot Press.

Recipe on page 134 by Ed Martley, from *Cooking Alaskan* © 1983, is reprinted by permission of Alaska Northwest Books, an imprint of Graphic Arts Center Publishing Co.

Project Editor: Tracee Williams
Layout: Maggie Peterson
Text Design: Elizabeth Kingsbury

Library of Congress Cataloging-in-Publication data is on file.

ISBN 978-0-7627-9175-0

Printed in the United States of America
10 9 8 7 6 5 4 3 2 1

To the memory of Gary Cox, chilihead

Contents

Part Four: Using and Serving Chili, 171

Introduction

Chili is simply a meat stew defined by chile peppers. Indeed, the early Spanish name for the dish was *chile con carne*—chiles with meat. That old name doesn't quite say it all, but it comes pretty close. Using lots of mild dried chile peppers and plenty of meat is the key to a superior and authentic chili. It's the chile pepper bulk that counts, not the heat; consequently, the chile pepper (mild kinds) should be considered a substantial ingredient, not just a spice. Unfortunately, however, the chile pepper has tended to diminish in importance as our chili recipes have become longer and longer, with more and more nonessential ingredients being added to the list.

It's true that a good bowl of chili isn't completely ruined by the addition of a little of this and a pinch of that. The real stuff stands up pretty well. What really bothers me, however, is what's being *left out* of some modern recipes. It's also true that modern concoctions can retain a certain taste (primarily from cumin, a latecomer to the list of essential ingredients) without the use of lots of dried chile pulp or pure chile powder—but the chili loses its strength and its soul.

If used in sufficient plenty, dried red chile peppers (usually in powdered form) add flavor, nutrition, bulk, and a certain smooth texture to chili. Moreover, it's the chile pepper, not the tomato, that puts the deep color into an authentic bowl of red.

Fortunately for modern cooks, dried red chile peppers of one kind or another (to be discussed at some length in the second chapter) are becoming more widely available these days—even in some supermarkets and Walmarts—and this trend is almost certain to continue. These dried peppers have a rather long shelf life and a reasonable price if purchased in bulk. For those who don't want to start from scratch, pure chile powder is available, also by the pound or in small packages, from dozens of modern pepper varieties. In either case, we could well be on the verge of a renaissance in great home-cooked chili. I can only hope that this modest work will help light the way.

—*A. D. Livingston*

PART ONE

Chili Ways and Means

The inspiration for raising the bar on modern chili lies in the past. That's why this books starts off in chapter 1 on a historical note along with recipes for basic old-time chili that will not taste quite like our modern versions. I think the flavor and texture and color of the real stuff—made with only three or four essential ingredients—are important and should be experienced before we dump the vegetable garden and the spice rack into the pot.

Fortunately, the scheme for this book allows us to start cooking in the first chapter instead of bogging down in a hundred pages of introductory stuff. More than once this approach has gotten me into difficulties with editors and people in the book business, causing one female critic to say that a cookbook of mine was about as organized as a bachelor's closet. So, be prepared to rummage around a little. Maybe you'll run across a surprise or uncover a secret here and there.

Chapter 2 is simply a primer on chile peppers, which I think is necessary for a modern chili book because dozens of varieties are becoming readily available to home cooks across the land for the first time. How exactly the chapter fits into the book's organization is difficult to explain and impossible to defend, except to say that it ought to go somewhere up front. It's simply too detailed for the introduction, however, and doesn't serve my agenda very well if it's forced into chapter 1. So, it's chapter 2. Personally, I think it follows naturally from chapter 1, where a case is made for returning the chile to our chili, but my critics may disagree. In any case, I hope that my recipe on making chili from scratch—that is, from whole dried red peppers, not from powder—will save the day.

Chapter 3 contains some important topics of contention for those few of us who like to be a little fussy about chili cooking details, along with some basics for those jacklegs amongst us who don't know how to simmer a stew and end up boiling it or, worse, scorching it. Of course, to boil chili vigorously is a cardinal sin.

Chapters 4 and 5 should present no special problems and need no explanation here, but chapter 6 might require comment. I won't mount an outright defense of this chapter, except to say that it is quite detailed and I admit to allowing it to run on somewhat unchecked. This seems to be the best way I can reflect the chaotic state of modern chili, in which almost anything and everything goes into the pot. Merely saying this is not enough. I need to hammer it in, nail by nail—wielding each small blow with clenched teeth and a wry smile. Who will fail to be a little amused to find that a contestant in a modern chili cook-off put prunes into the pot?

1

REDISCOVERING CHILI

Many are the theories and stories about the origins of chili. My favorite one concerns a beautiful and mysterious holy lady reported to have preceded the Spanish missionaries into northern Mexico, apparently to prepare the Native Americans for things to come. She was dressed in blue. This figure may have been Mary of Agreda, a nun in an order that called for blue dress. Trouble is, Sister Mary never left her convent in Spain. In the early 1600s, however, she was said to go into trances for several days and awaken with vivid memories of foreign lands. This has been described as an out-of-body experience. After one such visit to the New World, she reportedly wrote down a recipe the Native Americans had given to her. It consisted simply of venison, chile peppers, tomatoes, and onions, all simmered together in a clay pot. That's it.

Whether it be fact or fancy, I'll have to say here that Sister Mary's recipe contains a good deal of truth and reflects what I like to call the lost soul of modern chili. The Indians had the peppers and the venison and it would be unreasonable to believe that they wouldn't have combined the two, along with some wild onion. What could be more logical for a Mexican peasant recipe, far from the sophisticated Aztec cookery of Tenochtitlán (now Mexico City, where another version of early chili is said to have been made with chile peppers, tomatoes, and the meat of scrawny Spanish explorers)?

In any case, Sister Mary gave us a simple and probably authentic recipe from the peasant Indians of northern Mexico, regardless of how exactly it was transmitted over land and sea. Another version of the Mary of Agreda recipe, however, omits the tomatoes, but calls for some fat from wild hogs. Even today many people insist that fat is an essential ingredient in a bowl of chili, and I tend to agree. (Because the Indians had no real hogs, my guess is that the fat was from the javelina or peccary, a piglike critter that still roams the area in loose herds.) Already, you see, we have a controversy over the exact ingredients used for chili, and, of course, the Indians might well have argued amongst themselves on whether the tomato was a fitting ingredient for a bowl of red. In any case, we'll have a much more elaborate version of the Mary of Agreda recipe—also said to be authentic—later in the book.

Meanwhile, here are some other early chili recipes to try, not merely for historical purposes but to get back to the real stuff, pure and uncluttered. All the simple recipes in this chapter can produce a very good chili—but if you want the results to taste like what most people expect of chili these days, read the comments about cumin in chapter 4 and add some to taste.

A few of the recipes call for ancho or New Mexico chile peppers. These are large, mild peppers commonly used in chili and will be discussed in greater detail in the next chapter.

Indian Chile Con Carne

I've seen a number of Native American recipes, but most of them don't ring true, containing all manner of European spices and ingredients. Here's one adapted from American Indian Cooking: Recipes from the Southwest. *I think the recipe is very close to the original chili as cooked before the ancho-type chiles of that area were brought from Mexico into the Southwest by the Spanish, and it is very similar to the Mary of Agreda recipe. It is made with powdered chile and the cooking sequence is unusual.*

    game meat
    powdered red chile peppers (mild)
    garlic juice (optional)
    salt and pepper to taste

Cut some meat into chunks, put it into a pot, and cover with water, along with a little salt and pepper. Cook until the meat is tender, stirring from time to time and adding enough water to maintain a thin gravy. Remove the meat from the pot and slowly stir in enough powdered red chile to thicken and color the gravy. Return the meat to the gravy and heat through. Add a little garlic juice if wanted. (The pre-Columbian Indians did have wild garlic and wild onions, both quite strong by today's standards. Instead of using garlic juice, mince a little wild onion or garlic and add it in with the meat.)

Original Texas Chili

An early recipe for "Texas Chili" was set forth in 1828 by J. C. Clopper, who was visiting San Antonio at that time. It wasn't called chili, however. To paraphrase Clopper, the poor people of San Antonio would cut the meat into small chunks, add as many peppers, more or less, as there were pieces of meat, and stew the whole down until tender. There was no mention of spices. So . . . there's your first recipe for Texas chili, adapted here from The Chile Pepper Encyclopedia *by Dave DeWitt. It's not a bad chili, if you'll add a little salt.*

New Mexico Red

This recipe, which contains no European spices, has been adapted from Venison Cookery. *This is a committee-type cookbook with a dozen editors and photographers and food stylists listed in the front matter. It's much better than most such books, and deserves an author. Anyhow, the recipe was billed as "New Mexican–style chili," explaining that it has only a few ingredients and relies on dried chile pepper "to create a rich, gravy-like sauce." Unlike the other recipes in this chapter, the chiles are roasted before being used.*

1½ pound venison
1 ounce dried New Mexico reds
1 ounce dried ancho chiles
¾ cup chopped onions
4–6 cloves garlic, minced
1 teaspoon salt
water

Cut the venison into ½-inch cubes. Preheat the oven to 400°F. Remove the stem, inner membrane, and seeds from the peppers. Quickly rinse the peppers, then arrange them in a single layer on a large baking sheet (making two batches if necessary). Roast in the center of the oven for 5 minutes. Chop the peppers and put them into a food processor. Add the onion, garlic, salt, and ½ cup water. Pulse until the contents are finely chopped. Add the mixture to a suitable pot, preferably a cast-iron stovetop Dutch oven. While the water heats to a boil, add the venison cubes to the pot, reduce the heat, and simmer (do not boil) uncovered for about 30 minutes, or until the meat is tender and the chili is as thick as you like it. Serve hot.

Venison Cookery recommends that the chili be served with tortilla chips or over corn bread. It also recommends using the chili as a sauce over cheese–filled tortillas. Sounds good to me.

A. D.'s Stir-and-Taste Chili

Using a pure chile paste makes a good bowl of red if you like the cook, stir, and taste technique. Here's what you'll need, although you can add tomatoes, onions, and so on if you please. You can make your own chile paste (see chapter 2) or purchase some from stores and mail-order outfits that sell chile stuff.

> ground meat
> chile paste (preferably ancho or New Mexico)
> spices, if wanted
> water
> salt

Cook the meat in a little water, stirring until it turns gray and all the lumps are broken up. Add some chile paste. Cook, stir, and taste. Add more chile paste along with a few spices if wanted. Cook, stir, and taste. Add more chile paste, along with more water if needed, and salt to taste. Cook, stir, and taste until you have the chili the way you want it in flavor, texture, and color. Thus, each batch is made to taste, without a recipe or measures of ingredients. Maybe that's the way chili should be made.

2

CHILES FOR CHILI

Although the words "chili" and "chile" are often assumed to be interchangeable, and are so defined in some modern dictionaries, there can be a big and importance difference in meaning, as, for example, between the terms "chile powder" and "chili powder." Missing either term in a recipe, or failing to communicate with the cook, can completely alter the results. Half a cup of chili powder is simply not the same as half a cup of chile powder. To avoid confusion, I think it's best to define a few terms before going deeper into the cookery.

Chile, Chile Pepper (Plural, Chiles). A capsicum pepper plant, native to the New World, and the fruit thereof. The term "chile pepper" is technically redundant, but I find it useful and less jarring than "chile" if used in proximity to "chili." There are now over 200 varieties scattered around the globe, some mild, some hot, some very hot. (The other type of capsicum. usually called sweet pepper or bell pepper, is very mild and usually plays no defining role in making chili, although it is sometimes used as an ingredient.) Some chiles are 12 inches long, some only ½ inch. Large dried red chiles of mild hotness make up the bulk of those used in making "a bowl of red." Some of these chiles, such as ancho, have a thin meat, which allows them to sun-dry on the stalk in the field.

Green chiles are fresh vegetables (or fruits) and are required for making green chili. Note that the name of a chile in question sometimes changes from one form to another, depending on whether it is fresh and green or dried and red. Note also that a "green chile" can be red during the last part of its life. After it turns red, however, it dies and starts to dry out; its chemistry changes, including the vitamin content.

Chili. A stew made primarily of meat and dried red chile peppers. The latter ingredient can take several forms, including powdered chiles with spices and a paste made with dried chiles. The term is sometimes spelled "chilli" in the Midwest, reportedly due to a misspelling in a café window, and in Australia. A stew made from meat and green chile peppers should properly be called "green chili" or "green chili stew."

Chile Powder. Sometimes called "chile molido" in some recipes, this is pure chile powder made from grinding dry red chiles, without any spice or other additives. It can be made at home or purchased in small packages or in bulk, by the pound. Dozens of kinds are available, with ancho and New Mexico chile powder being more popular for making chili.

Chili Powder. A spice mixture or seasoning made with chile powder, ground cumin, and other spices. In commercial chili powders, the ingredients are listed on the package in the order of importance based on volume.

Chili Mixes. A mix of chile powder, cumin, and other spices, along with other ingredients such as flour or masa harina. Often the ingredients are packaged in a box or bag with two or three pouches of ingredients. The ingredients for the whole mix are usually listed on the main package in the order of importance based on volume. A recipe and instructions are included for most mixes. There are hundreds of these, available mostly by mail order. Some are sold in supermarkets and grocery stores, sometimes in the spice section and sometimes in the section that sells packets of gravy mixes and such. Several of these mixes are discussed in chapter 4, along with recipes for using them.

Chile con Carne. Sometimes called carne con chile, this is an old Spanish term that is often used to denote chili. Literally, the term means "meat with chile peppers." Sometimes we see "chile con carne with beans," which is a very useful term if the chili contains beans.

Chili con Carne. Same as chile con carne.

Carne con Chile. Same as chile con carne.

A Bowl of Red. Slang for a bowl of chili. It does have much meaning, however, for those who know their stuff. Some so-called chili isn't red at all, and some is colored by tomatoes. In the real stuff the red comes from sun-dried chile peppers. Or damn well should.

Capsaicin. This is the stuff that makes chile peppers hot. In each pepper, up to 80 percent of its capsaicin is in the seeds and inner veins. Therefore, removing the seeds and veins (the pithy stuff inside) will turn a hot chile into a rather mild one. Proper handling for hot peppers is discussed later in this chapter. Be warned here that capsaicin oil can burn your eyes and private parts.

Scoville Unit. This is the unit of measure used by the food industry to classify the hotness of chile peppers, using the Scoville scale. The mild bell peppers, sweet bananas, and a few others rank 0 or almost 0. This goes up to about 5,000 units for the familiar jalapeño—and up to a whopping 500,000 units for the habanero and a few others.

RED CHILE PRIMER

There are dozens of kinds of chile peppers that can be used for chili, but the field is somewhat narrowed by a practical consideration: Mild peppers are normally used for the bulk of the chile content, with a small amount of hot pepper often added for spice. The seeds of milder peppers are also used for heat.

Anyhow, here are a few peppers commonly used for making chili. Note the absence of such favorites as cayenne, Tabasco, and bell peppers. All of these can be used in one way or another, but they are simply not important in the world of chili.

Ancho. Measuring in at 1,000 to 1,500 on the Scoville scale, the poblano—the green form of the ancho pepper—is one of the more popular chiles in Mexico. It's a large, rather heart-shaped pepper, measuring 5 inches long and 3 inches across the top. When sun-dried, the ancho is a deep, reddish brown and is relatively sweet, permitting it to be used in some quantity without making the dish too hot to eat. Consequently, these peppers are widely used in chili and chili powder as well as in the many Mexican *moles*. Anchos are available in many markets and by mail order in bulk (by the pound), in powdered form, and in flakes (sometimes called chile caribe).

Confusingly, the pepper is sometimes called pasilla and several other names in Mexico and the United States.

New Mexico Chiles. These are descendants, now available in dozens of varieties, of the Mexican peppers that the Spanish brought into the Southwest from points south. It's a long chile (8 inches or more) measuring only 500 to 1,000 on the Scoville scale, making it a good choice for chili. It is often used in decorative ristras. These make good props for Western movies, but they are not always good culinary choices because they are sometimes sprayed with various preservatives or coatings.

New Mexico peppers are available in bulk (by the pound) as well as powdered form and flakes. Anyone who lives in New Mexico and Arizona, and parts of California, may have a wider choice in varieties—and some regional recipes specify such varieties as New Mexico Number 6, NuMex Big Jim, and so on—but most of us will have to be content with whatever varieties we can find in local markets and by mail order. Home gardeners now have a good selection of seeds from which to choose.

In general, the early New Mexico peppers were rather hot, and the trend has always been to find a milder pepper, a larger pepper, and one that matures earlier. In any case, the chile is a major crop in New Mexico, which has about 30,000 acres in cultivation, with much agricultural and horticultural research and development under way.

Anaheim. This is the commercial name given to an early variety of New Mexico chile grown in the Anaheim area of California. In northern Mexico, an Anaheim in the dried stage is called a colorado chile; in the green stage, chile verde. When the green Anaheim is roasted, skinned, and dried, it becomes a pasado chile.

Pasilla Negro. Several chiles are called *pasilla,* and the heat level varies considerably. In some places, the ancho is called *pisilla*—and in Mexico "pasilla" is also applied to the darker ancho chiles. Further, pasilla is sometimes called *anchocolarado* in parts of Mexico. In general, the pasilla negro is a long, cylindrical chile with a dark color and a fruity, coffee flavor. It is often used in Mexican cooking, especially for making moles and adobo sauces. For chili, the pasilla is usually used in dried form as a minor supplement to ancho or New Mexico chiles. The New Mexico chiles were probably developed from pasilla chiles.

The *pasilla oaxaqueño* variety, raised in Oaxaca, Mexico, is much hotter than the pasilla negro, and is usually smoke-dried. It ranks between 5,000 and 15,000 on the Scoville scale. The pasilla negro, by comparison, places between 1,000 and 1,500 units—the same as the ancho.

Jalapeño. This popular hot pepper can add heat to a bowl of red, but it is not of the essence. Often it is used as a go-with or topping. The pepper is meaty and doesn't sun-dry properly. When smoke-dried, it is usually called chipotle. For smoke-dried jalapeños, read on.

Chipotle. Broadly, this term refers to smoke-dried peppers, a current rage in some culinary circles. Actually, smoke-drying peppers is a very old practice, predating the Aztecs. As a rule, only peppers with a thick meat are smoke-dried, whereas thin peppers are usually sun-dried. In other words, the process was originally a means of preservation.

By far the most popular smoke-dried pepper in the United States is the jalapeño, which (when smoked) is now called chipotle in recipes and culinary works. These are usually smoke-dried in the red stage, but they turn a drab grayish tan during the smoking and drying. The flavor is distinctive—sweetish with a hint of chocolate and tobacco, but on the hot side. The heat scale is the same as the regular jalapeño, between 5,000 and 10,000 Scoville units. They are available in bulk dried form, as well as in flakes and powder, and canned chipotle chiles are widely available in supermarkets. I like the bulk dried pods for use in chili.

In Mexico, these peppers have several names, depending in part on how long they are smoked. Also jalapeños smoke-dried in the green stage are called *jalapeño chico,* whereas a *japone* is a smoke-dried red jalapeño. And so on. It is safe to assume the chipotle peppers called for in modern recipes are smoke-dried jalapeños, unless otherwise specified.

Other smoke-dried peppers are also available, including the superhot habanero. Use any of these with caution.

Chile de Arbol. This is a popular red chile in Mexico and is often used to make chile powder similar to cayenne but not quite as hot. It is rather hot, however—between 15,000 and 30,000 on the Scoville scale—and makes a good chile to add heat and color to a bowl of red. It grows on a bush that resembles a small tree. The pods grow to 2 or 3 inches in length and about ½ inch in diameter.

Other Chiles. Interesting peppers are now grown in Thailand, Africa, and other parts of the world, where they have greatly influenced the local cuisine. Only the French and the Eskimos seem to have escaped the taste of hot capsicum peppers. All of these were developed from the American peppers found by the Spanish explorers. Often these are quite hot and are used primarily to add heat to chili and other dishes. The hottest, the habanero, ranks from 100,000 to over 300,000 on the Scoville scale. (Note that some books on chili and chile peppers—even some published in modern times—give incorrect information on peppers, stating that the small wild peppers are the hottest species and that small peppers with pointed ends are the hottest. The habanero and its cousins, such as the Scotch bonnet, don't fit either description.)

My personal favorite among the hot peppers is the wild piquin pepper, which rates between 30,000 and 50,000—the same as the familiar cayenne, Tabasco, and chiletepin. Several wild peppers around the world are called bird peppers because the seeds are dropped by birds, thereby spreading the plant. Most of these wild peppers are on the small side. Some grow wild in the United States, mostly in the Southwest and sparsely along the coastal plain to Florida, where they thrive in and around some orange groves.

An interesting group of peppers—the *aji*—are grown in Peru and other parts of South America. There are more than a dozen kinds, and, of course, a species is likely to have several popular names.

Clearly, a complete discourse on chiles would have to be very long, and would be more than most people want to know—and certainly more than they need know for cooking up an outstanding bowl of red. My best advice is this: Stick to the well-known heat scale, color, and taste of the ancho and the New Mexico chiles.

Add any of the others in small amounts for heat and table discussion. Treat the habanero types—and there are several, including the Florida datil pepper and the Caribbean Scotch bonnet—as a hazardous substance. Rubber gloves and protective breathing masks are in order.

Dried Chile How-To

I have read that dried red peppers should be skinned—but I don't see how. Green chiles can be roasted and skinned, but it doesn't work with dried peppers, at least not for me. If I try to devein and skin a dry red chile, I don't have anything left.

Reconstituting Dried Chiles. Simply soak dried red peppers in water for several hours or overnight. Some people, and I am one, may want to save the soaking water for use in the recipe.

Controlling the Heat. Most of the heat-producing capsaicin in a chile pepper will be in the inner pith and seeds, as stated earlier. Properly removing these parts will reduce the heat by at least 80 percent. The pith and seeds can be removed while the chiles are dry, or after they have been reconstituted by soaking in water. It's probably best to devein in the dry stage, but I confess that I usually do it after soaking.

Removing the seeds and pith is easy. Simply cut off the stem end of the pepper and split the pod open. Using your finger or perhaps a small spoon or knife, get out the seeds, core, and veins. Also remember that oil of capsaicin can burn your eyes and private parts, and even ordinary skin. So, wash your hands after seeding and deveining peppers. Prissies wear rubber gloves.

Some people save the seeds of dried peppers for use as a spice, to add heat to chili and other dishes. The Native Americans burned the seeds as a fumigant to rid the lodge of bedbugs.

Red Pepper Flakes. Crumbled red peppers are often used as a spice to add heat to foods. Rather generic red pepper flakes can be purchased in any supermarket, and various kinds can be found in spice catalogs. Also, dried red peppers, such as cayenne, can be crumbled on the spot. I am fond of the little wild bird peppers, used sparingly. Try crumbling a pod or two in a pot of pinto beans during the cooking phase. Or add to the water in which rice is to be cooked. Pepper flakes can also be used to kick up a pizza or salad.

Pure Chile Powders

Usually, sun-dried red chiles are not quite dry enough to be powdered. First, remove the seeds, core, and inner veins (if you want a mild powder). Place the deveined peppers on a flat pan and heat in an oven at about 300°F, or until they start to brown. Or heat them on a griddle. In either case, be careful not to burn the chiles. Cool and place them in a blender or food mill, zapping them until you have a fine powder. Sift this if you want to get out any red specs from the skin. Be warned that dust from chiles can cause breathing problems. If you grind them in a fast mill, it's best to wear a painter's mask.

Store the chile powder in an airtight container in a cool, dark place. But it's best not to grind more than you need simply because, like coffee and black pepper, freshly ground chile has more flavor.

Although freshly ground red chile pepper is best, most people would prefer to buy the powder from a reputable dealer. It's cheaper by the pound, but smaller packages might be the way to go unless you use lots of it. Some dealers offer a wide variety of chile powders, so that the compleat chilihead can mix several kinds.

I think it's best to use this chile powder as an ingredient, adding various spices to the recipe separately. But others will want to mix ground spices in with the chile powder—making a chili powder. Hundreds of chili powders and chili mixes are available commercially. Some of these are discussed in chapter 4, as well as notes and recipes for making your own mix.

RED CHILE PASTES

It's easy to make a chile paste if you've got a good electric blender. Simply soak dried red peppers overnight in water, stem and seed them, and put them into a blender. Add a little olive oil and zap them until you have a smooth paste. Strain the paste to get out any flecks of skin, if you want to remove them.

It's even easier to order chile paste by mail. Some offer a pure paste made from ancho and a dozen other chiles, available in cans or jars of several sizes. Of course, the compleat chilihead will want to mix several chile pastes to taste, by color and possibly by heat.

It's easy to make chili simply by browning some ground meat and stirring in some chile paste to taste, along with some onions and tomatoes and spices. Being easy to stir into the pot, paste can also be used to adjust chili made with powder.

GREEN CHILE PRIMER

Green chile is becoming more popular these days, partly because fresh chile peppers are more widely available in supermarkets and by mail order. Also, home gardeners are learning how to grow a variety of green peppers. Often several kinds of green chiles are used in a single recipe, some for bulk and some to heat and flavor. Generally, the favorite kinds for making green chili include these:

Poblano. This important Mexican chile is dark green and has a rather mild flavor, although the heat scale varies quite a bit. It's a large pepper, measuring 4 or 5 inches long and up to 3 inches wide at the top, tapering off to a point at the bottom, giving it an odd triangular or heart shape. The mature poblano turn a reddish brown color and is sweeter than the green form. (When mature and dried, the poblano is called the ancho pepper, widely used in red chili, as discussed under red peppers above.) Although it grows best in Mexico and the southwestern United States, I can grow an acceptable poblano in my Florida garden. The poblano is available fresh in Mexican markets during summer and fall, and is increasingly seen in upscale supermarkets. The poblano is also available canned.

New Mexico. The modern New Mexico green chiles are varieties that have been developed from Mexican chiles brought north by the Spanish. Sometimes called Anaheim (covered under the next heading), there are now dozens of varieties with some emphasis on size and controlled heat level. The NuMex Big Jim, for example, grows up to 12 inches long and has a medium heat. One of the earliest of these chiles was dubbed New Mexico Number 9, followed by a New Mexico Number 6, which matured earlier and resisted wilt. Anyone interested in the agricultural development of these peppers should peruse *The Chile Pepper Encyclopedia* by Dave DeWitt. Most of these peppers are grown in New Mexico, Arizona, and California, as well as south of the border. Note also that seeds of the modern varieties are available from the garden supply houses.

In any case, New Mexico green chiles are available fresh in some markets that traffic in southwestern ingredients as well as in some supermarkets. Canned New Mexico green chiles are also available.

Anaheim. This is a variety of New Mexico chile, named for the California town where it was first grown. The Anaheim is common in some American markets, and is available fresh or canned. Because it is mild and large—up to 8 inches long—the Anaheim is an excellent choice for green chili.

Jalapeño. This medium–hot pepper is widely available in supermarkets these days in fresh and canned form. It can be used in green chili, but, owing to its heat in comparison to the ancho and New Mexico chiles, it is a little too hot for comfort for most of us. I think it's best to seed and devein it very carefully before using it in large quantity.

Bell Peppers. Yes, these are varieties developed from capsicum chiles, but they have very little heat left. Usually, these are meatier than the other green peppers and are usually used in salads, pepper steak and stir-fry dishes, stuffed peppers, and so on, not in chili or green chili. Although they are usually very mild, in recent years hotter varieties have been forthcoming.

ROASTED GREEN PEPPERS

Roasting green peppers can be accomplished on a gas stove burner, exposing the pepper directly to the heat of the flame, or on an indoor grill such as the Jenn-Air. It's really best, however, to use an outdoor grill, preferably heated with hardwood or charcoal. A little smoke helps. In any case, heat the peppers until they are blackened, then turn and blacken the other side. The idea is to blister the pepper's skin, making it easy to remove. When all sides are blackened, put the peppers into a paper bag for 10 minutes or a little longer. Then carefully scrape the skin off the peppers with a small knife, rinsing under running water as you go. A few specks of black left on the peppers here and there won't hurt a thing. After the skin has been removed, cut off the stem end. Remove the seeds and the inner core. Rinse the peppers and set aside. For use in chili, simply dice the peppers or puree them in a food processor, or follow the directions in the recipes.

Chili From Scratch

I can't leave this chapter without setting forth a recipe for cooking
a bowl of modern chili from scratch. This takes more time—but
I think the results are worth the effort and ought to be fun for
white-hat chefs as well as for culinary sports. The recipe is a little
more complex than those in chapter 1, and it tastes more like modern chili, owing to the cumin, which is ground from whole seeds as
needed. This practice gives a better flavor, I think, than using store-
bought cumin powder, which goes stale quicker than the whole
seeds.

A. D.'s Range Cow Chile

*Here's a recipe that I like to make from dried chile peppers and some cumin
for flavor, without going the chili powder route. No powder is used, except
a little cayenne for heat. I think the whole peppers lend a better texture to
the chili.*

The Chili Paste

  ½ pound dried ancho or New Mexico chile peppers
  ¼ pound smoke-dried chipotle chile peppers
  2–3 dried japone chile peppers
  powdered cayenne to taste
  2 tablespoons whole cumin seeds (or more)
  1 tablespoon sea salt
  springwater

Soak the peppers in water for several hours, or overnight. Drain
the peppers, saving some of the water. Split the peppers in half

lengthwise, and cut off the stem ends. Remove the seeds and inner pith or ribs (which is where most of the heat is), placing the peppers into a blender as you go. In a cast-iron skillet, toast the cumin seeds for a few minutes, then grind them with a mortar and pestle. Add the ground cumin to the blender, along with the sea salt and a little of the reserved pepper water. Pulse the mix several times until you have a smooth, deeply red paste. Appreciate the color and you'll know why chili is often called "a bowl of red." Add a little cayenne to adjust the heat, if needed, and add more cumin if necessary to fulfill your taste for the stuff. This can be done now or toward the end of the cooking period.

THE MEAT

5 pounds tough beef, diced
¼ pound smoked bacon, diced
chili paste (from above recipe)
freshly ground black pepper to taste
fine white cornmeal (stone ground)
springwater or beef stock

Fry the bacon in a stovetop cast-iron Dutch oven or other suitable pot until it is crisp. (If you want to avoid the animal fat, skip the bacon and use a little vegetable oil in the pot.) Add the beef and lightly brown. Stir in the chili paste. Add about 2 cups of water or beef stock. Bring to a light boil, reduce the heat to low, cover tightly, and simmer for 2 hours, stirring and adding more water from time to time as needed. Taste and add more salt if needed and, maybe, an additional pinch or two of cumin. Stirring as you go, sprinkle on some cornmeal, about ¼ cup, to thicken or "tighten" the chili. Cook, stir, and taste, adding more of this or that, until you get it right. Toward the end, add some freshly ground black pepper to taste, if wanted.

Serve the chili hot in wide bowls, along with suitable go-withs, including beans, chopped onions, scallions, tomatoes, rice, pasta, Texas toothpicks (slivers of jalapeño peppers), sliced jícama, sour cream, grated cheese, coleslaw, and so on, as discussed in chapter 18. Many people want pinto or red kidney beans with their chili. Even heated canned beans will do, but they tend to be a little too mushy (especially if cooked again with the chili). Other kinds of beans can also be used.

Note carefully that such go-withs as beans, onions, and chopped tomatoes are not necessarily put into the pot of chili during or after cooking. Instead, each bowl of red is fixed separately with whatever go-withs the individual partaker wants, either as a side dish or as a topping for the bowl. That way, any chili left in the pot is pure and freezes nicely. Leftovers can be used in tacos, tamales, and so on—even on Italian pasta, al dente, of course. In fact, chili on pasta is traditional in parts of the Midwest, especially around Cincinnati.

Saltine crackers or oyster crackers are traditional for chili and are sometimes crumbled into the bowl. Rolled cornmeal tortillas are excellent with chili, as are corn chips. Other go-with suggestions are set forth in chapter 18.

3

TOOLS AND TECHNIQUES FOR COOKING AND USING CHILI

Most kitchen stoves, either gas or electric, will do for making a small pot of chili. For large batches, however, the real chilihead may want to consider an outdoor unit designed for boiling crabs or frying a whole turkey. Ideal for the patio or camp, most of these burn propane gas from 20-pound rechargeable cylinders, but other rigs are also available, and pots are available in several sizes. There are several advantages to these rigs, not the least of which is easy heat control (with a valve regulating the flow of gas to the burner).

In general, it's best to avoid a charcoal or wood fire unless the pot is suspended above the heat and can be easily and safely elevated or lowered, or swung away from the heat to control the boil. Trying to remove a large pot from a grill or grid can be dangerous.

Anyhow, here's my take on cooking utensils and a few other handy items for making chili:

Pots. A rule of thumb is to use a heavy pot for simmering meat in a liquid. Thick pots dissipate the heat better and aren't as likely to burn the bottom of the food. Thin pots work all right for boiling crabs for a few minutes or cooking pasta al dente, where lots of liquid is used and the bottom of the food isn't likely to burn. I prefer a cast-iron stovetop Dutch oven, but many chiliheads prefer stainless steel, especially in the large pots designed to fit over outdoor propane burners. A few chiliheads and other cooks warn against using aluminum pots, however, for long simmering.

It is very important for the pot to have a tight-fitting lid, usually dome shaped. Such a lid will be cooler than the bottom of the pot and will condense the water vapor that arises during cooking. The condensation drips back into the pot, saving you the trouble of constantly adding water. Thus, a really good pot with a tight lid will cook for hours without a problem, whereas a thin pot with a loosely fitted lid requires constant attention.

Crock-Pots. The old Crock-Pots with the heating elements spiraled around the sides instead of coiled in the bottom are great for making chili. It's almost always best to fill the Crock-Pot almost to the top, no matter what you are cooking. Simply put in all the ingredients, cover, and cook on low for 7 or 8 hours without peeking or stirring. Remove the cover, stir, taste, add seasonings as needed, cover again, and cook for another hour or so. Some people will brown the meat in a skillet before putting it into the pot, but this usually isn't necessary.

Pressure Cookers. These are good to have on hand, but their main purpose is to cook food quickly, a notion at odds with the philosophy of most chiliheads. Pressure cookers work, however, and a recipe calling for 2 pounds of ground meat, along with canned beans and tomatoes, onions, and other ingredients, can be cooked in 6 minutes. In short, all you do is put all the ingredients into the pot, bring it to a boil, set the pressure, and cook it the prescribed length of time, following the directions that came with your cooker. Personally, I am more likely to use my pressure cooker as a handy pot, without the pressure mechanism engaged. Suit yourself.

Skillets. Most skillets of reasonable size can be used to make a small batch of chili. Heavy skillets work best for long, slow cooking, and I am partial to cast iron. Thin skillets tend to burn food on the bottom. The auxiliary electrically heated skillets are handy for chili and simmer nicely, partly because of the easy heat control.

Meat Grinders. Although most chili recipes call for regular hamburger meat, the better choice is to use a coarser grind—especially if the chili is to be simmered for a long time. The one exception is chili sauce for hot dogs, in which a very fine grind works better. In short, it's best for the chilihead to grind his own meat. Several kinds of inexpensive grinders are available, either electric or hand-cranked. Choose one that uses a wide selection of cutting wheels and blades, and (why not?) one that has a sausage stuffing attachment available. I think you will find that your chili and your hamburger taste better if you grind your own meat, partly because you'll know exactly what's in it. Deer hunters especially will benefit from a kitchen grinder.

Flame Tamers. These can be one of the most important items for the chilihead who likes to simmer his chili all day without constant attention. Available for electric or gas kitchen ranges, they help keep the heat very low so that the chili simmers instead of boils. This, in turn, helps keep the water in the pot, and prevents the bottom from scorching. Some stoves need these badly; others don't.

Knives. Although long butcher knives are required for slicing large chunks of meat, a small, sharp knife really works best for dicing meat that has been cut at the market into steaks, chops, or other slabs. A 6-inch paring knife will do, especially if it has an ordinary carbon steel blade. A good whetstone with true grit is the best and most satisfying way to sharpen a small knife.

The Chili Stick. Many cooks, especially cook-off enthusiasts and patio sports, prefer to stir their chili with wood paddles or sticks. Paddles with a square end work best for dredging up the bottom, where bits are likely to stick. Even skillet cooks will do better to stir with a wooden spoon or spatula, especially with a cast-iron skillet. Metal to metal makes a scraping noise and tends to scratch up the nonstick surface of the skillet or pot. In any case, true chiliheads won't allow their chili stick to be used for stirring anything else.

COOKING STRATEGIES

A gallon of chili is good to have, but 2 gallons are twice as good, especially because chili is better the second or third day and because it freezes well. For that reason alone, cooking a large pot of chili usually makes sense, especially if you like to spend half a day on the project. The long, slow simmering almost always results in a better bowl of red.

In some cases, however, a quicker chili may be in order, in which case you may opt to cook only a small batch in a skillet. With most recipes these days you can simply put everything into a pot along with some water, bring it to a boil, cover, and cook for as long as you like, stirring from time to time and adding water as needed. But there can be more to it than that. Here are some thoughts on the matter.

Brown and Serve. Here's what I call a quick supermarket chili. Brown a pound of hamburger meat in a skillet. Add a can of beans and a can of tomatoes, along with a tablespoon of chili powder. Cook for 10 minutes and serve hot with crackers. It's quick. It's easy. And it isn't bad, either.

Browning the Meat. Many recipes for chili start with cooking the ground meat, usually in a little oil, until it turns gray. The real purpose here is not to "brown" the meat, as the saying goes, but to break up any chunks of meat. The purpose of the oil is to keep the meat from sticking to the pot or skillet at the start of the cooking. Note also that this phrase should not be taken literally.

Cooking the meat until it is gray, or loses its redness, will do in most recipes—but I find the phrase "gray the meat" simply doesn't work. Hence, it's still "brown the meat."

The Long Simmer. Tough meat simmered for a long time at low temperature makes the best chili and gives the cook the satisfaction of making a tasty dish from a cheaper cut of meat. It also allows the cook plenty of time for sniffing, tasting, and stirring, adding a little of this or that ingredient as needed to season the perfect bowl of red while also enjoying a few beers.

Cooking in the Stock. Chili that is thinned with stock has more depth than that cooked with plain water. Sometimes stock and water are mixed about half and half. Much depends on how much water the ingredients contain, such as tomato. Canned stock is usually specified in recipes, either beef or chicken. The best stocks however, are made at home and require soup bones, which are not often displayed these days in supermarkets.

I think the best bet is to cook a tough piece of meat that also contains some bone, such as beef or lamb shanks. The shanks are cooked until tender and boned. The bones are cut into segments or cracked and put back into the pot to cook out the marrow, which is part of the stock's secret. The meat is cubed and put back into the pot, along with the rest of the ingredients, and simmered some more. Many of the recipes in this book can be easily adapted for this approach to chili.

Reaching Critical Mass. I've always believed that a large cast-iron pot—say, a 4-quart Dutch oven—filled to almost an inch from the top makes the best chili. This isn't a matter of recipe; instead, it involves the deep and unexplained mysteries of a full pot. Perhaps a full pot simmers better at low heat, whereas a partly filled pot tends to be hotter.

SERVING CHILI

Most chili is served in a suitable bowl and eaten with a spoon. Various toppings can be added to the chili, preferably floated on top. If, for example, you are going to serve rice with the chili, don't put the rice into the bowl first. Instead, float a round dollop of white rice in the center of the bowl of red, making good use of the color of both. Side dishes can also be served on a plate beside the bowl, or passed around as needed. The best plan, I think, is to serve chili in large, heavy bowls with various toppings or go-withs and condiments put in the center of the table in bowls or containers, or perhaps on a lazy Susan. Make a spread. Maybe two or three kinds of beans. Salsa in mild, medium, and hot, and so on.

It is traditional in most parts of the country to serve crackers with chili, preferably saltines or oyster crackers. Chopped tomatoes, chopped onions, and shredded cheese are very popular with chili, either as a topping or on the side. In recent years, sour cream has become a standard offering with a bowl of red. Thus, the partakers can customize their chili according to their tastes and requirements. Suitable go-withs are discussed at more length in chapter 18. Often, however, an exact way to serve the chili is specified in the recipe. One such recipe, said to be Professional Chili by Paul Lastowski and Jackie Stevens, instructs us to add 1 teaspoon of sour cream to the center of the bowl of red. Squeeze on the juice of ¼ wedge of lime. Pour ½ shot of good tequila over the sour cream, and garnish with thin lime wedges.

A few recipes call for serving chili on a plate, usually as a topping for rice or pasta. Very thick chili can also be served on a plate, along with suitable go-withs, and eaten with a fork.

Widemouthed vacuum jars are suitable for the road or camp. Eat right out of the jar, using a large spoon.

LEFTOVERS

Many people claim that chili is better the second day, and I tend to agree. Leftovers can be heated and eaten like an ungarnished bowl of red, or they can be used to top spaghetti, rice, or hot dogs, and in other dishes as set forth in other chapters. You can also modify leftover chili in one way or another. For example, leftovers to be used for spaghetti sauce might be cooked a little longer with some additional tomato sauce or paste. I also like to brown a few onions in a skillet, then add some leftover chili. Or combine leftover chili and a can of beans. And so on.

The home vacuum-pack systems are great for freezing chili in plastic bags, but I really prefer to put mine up in small plastic containers of either 1 or 1½ cups. The 1-cup size is thawed out and heated (usually in the microwave) to make one serving of chili in a plate over a bed of rice or pasta. This lets me get out 1 cup for each partaker—as many as needed. The 1½-cup size is used for serving a single bowl of chili, with beans and go-withs provided separately, if wanted. I might add that the best chili for freezing contains no beans.

So . . . why not make a big pot of chili and freeze what you can't eat the first or second day? You'll be glad you did.

4

MODERN CHILI POWDERS AND MIXES

The dominating flavor in modern chili is cumin, an Old World spice that was brought to Mexico by the Spanish explorers. Some folks, however, maintain that cumin itself and the recipe for chili were brought directly to San Antonio, Texas, by immigrants from the Canary Islands, thus bypassing Mexico. What would Sister Mary say about that?

In any case, it seems clear that San Antonio figured largely in the development of chili as we now know it. Commercially, chili came of age there when young ladies, usually Mexican, started selling food to soldiers, travelers, and others, day and night, from crude stalls and carts in what was called El Mercado, a commercial market in the Military Plaza. Chili was an ideal food to sell because it required only an olla to cook and a bowl to serve, usually with rolled tortillas. In time the young ladies came to be known as Chili Queens. They live on even today in an annual reenactment in San Antonio called "Return of the Chili Queens Festival."

As soon as chili took hold, it spread to Mexican eateries in Texas and other parts of the country. At first the chili was made from scratch, but pure chile powder was marketed in Mexico's Valley of Oaxaca as early as 500 BC.

Once the chile powder was available commercially, it was an easy step to add cumin and other spices to the mix. These chili mixes were used more and more simply because they were convenient to store and use, and were ideal for the market. With these inexpensive mixes, chili could easily be made at home and on the range, far and wide.

Today we have hundreds of chili mixes and chili powders available from the supermarket, specialty markets, and by mail order. To help sort all this out, I divide commercial chili fixin's into the following three categories, although there is some overlap:

Supermarket Spice Shelf Chili Powders. These widely available chili powders are what many folks use to make most of America's family chili. Treated as a spice, these powders are usually sold in small jars or tins, often with a sprinkle top. They contain chile powder, cumin, and other ingredients, as listed on the package along with a chili recipe, usually calling for ground beef, canned tomatoes, and canned beans. Many cooks will add some more cumin and other spices, but they do not often add more of what's really needed for a good, thick bowl of red: pure chile powder. Lots of it.

Chili Mixes, Seasonings, and Blends. Often more elaborate than chili powder spice mixes, these products are usually packaged in cardboard boxes or little brown bags with a fold-over top. The chili mix itself is contained in a sealed plastic pouch. In supermarkets these mixes are usually displayed in a section containing gravy mixes and such, not in the spice section. Often the mix contains thickeners such as flour or masa harina, adding more bulk to the dump. A few of these are sold in supermarkets, sometimes on a regional basis, and many others are available by mail order or in specialty shops. As a rule, these are usually considered a cut above the chili spice mix. Of course, the compleat chilihead will want to mix both chili powder and chili mixes, and somehow feels compelled to add more cumin, oregano, and so on.

Most of these mixes will claim to be "the original" while at the same time appealing to the latest good ol' boy fad. For example, a popular mix in my neck of the woods, Lysander's, offers an original mix as well as separate bags dubbed hickory and mesquite. The package explains this with an ingredient called "hickory powder" or "mesquite powder." Note also that some of the larger spice outfits, such as McCormick, offer a chili seasoning as well as a chili powder; these usually contain pretty much the same ingredients, except that the seasoning contains a thickener such as flour or masa harina.

Chili Dumps. These are more elaborate than chili spices or mixes, and allow the cook more range for personalization. Packaged in paper bags or boxes, the typical dump contains a pouch of chile powder, cumin, and spices; a second pouch contains a little hot chile powder, giving the cook the option of using it to taste; and a third pouch contains masa harina, flour, or some such thickener. Some of these are available in supermarkets, often on a regional basis, but by far the widest selection is by mail order. In some versions, the ingredients of each dump are printed on the individual pouches. Recipes on the main package instruct us on when and how to use the dumps, and in what quantity for producing a two-alarm, three-alarm, or false-alarm chili. Often the language is entertaining, slanted for the most part toward beer-drinking good ol' boys.

A Few Fixin's to Try

Here are a few recipes making use of commercial chili mixes. Most of these brands can be purchased through mail-order outfits and sometimes in supermarkets.

Hell's Half Acre Chili

This recipe comes from Pendery's, an old Texas outfit that markets a number of chili blends, including the original Chil tomaline mix. This recipe, made with their Top Hat blend, has a deep red color; if the blend is used in sufficient quantity, it gives chili a full-bodied taste. The recipe has been adapted from a letter to the author from Mary Pendery Haggerty, whose grandfather, DeWitt Clinton Pendery, started the firm in 1870 near a section of Fort Worth called Hell's Half Acre.

6 pounds lean chuck (¾-inch grind or dice)
6 dried ancho chile pods
3–6 de arbol chile pods to taste (used whole)
24 level tablespoons Pendery's Top Hat chili blend
2 heads fresh garlic
½ tablespoon salt, or to taste
¼ teaspoon ground cumin
flour, if needed
boiling water

Separate the garlic heads. Peel the cloves and slice them into ⅟₁₆-inch slices. Discard the stem ends of the ancho chile pods, remove the seeds, and wash. (Leave the de arbol pods whole.) Place the coarsely ground or diced meat into a stovetop Dutch oven, preferably cast iron, with a tight-fitting lid. Pour in enough boiling water to barely cover the meat. Turn the heat to high until the water almost boils. Reduce the heat to low and simmer for 30 to 40 minutes. Skim off the fat (do this before the seasonings are added, Pendery's advises). Add the ancho pods and garlic, along with 3 to 6 whole de arbol chile pods. Simmer on very low heat—do not boil—for about 40 minutes, until the ancho meat has separated from the skins. Discard the skins. Discard the whole de arbol pods. Slowly add the Top Hot blend, stirring as you go, along with the salt and cumin. Simmer for another 25 minutes, stirring from time to time and adding a little boiling water as needed. Add a little flour to thicken the chili, if desired.

Pendery's says the flavor will be even better the second day. I agree. So, cook more than you need—and don't worry about the size of the servings. If you want to get rid of the hell part of the recipe, the firm says, simply omit the de arbol pods.

William Gephardt's Chili

William Gephardt, a German immigrant, started marketing a chili mix as early as 1890 in Texas. It's still going and is one of the more widely distributed mixes available. The Official Chili Book *says the current mix is exactly the same as the original—still held secret. (The exact measures may be secret, but remember that the ingredients of commercial products must be listed on the label or package in order by volume.) In any case, I've seen several recipes attributed to the Gephardt firm, and, of course, the brand is called for in many other chili recipes. As best I can tell, the firm slanted its recipes toward the lucrative Midwest market, using plenty of beans—in spite of the fact that this recipe is described as a "lusty Texas chili" in Bill Bridges'* The Great Chili Book! *Bridges adds that Gephardt's sets the standard by which other chili powders are judged. He also says to forget the beans if you want San Antonio–style chili.*

    1 pound ground beef
    1 (15-ounce) can Gephardt's Mexican-style beans or
        Gephardt's pinto beans (optional)
    3 cups tomato juice or water
    ½ small onion, chopped (optional)
    3¼ tablespoons Gephardt's Eagle Brand Chili Powder
    ⅓ cup flour
    1 teaspoon salt

Lightly brown the beef and onion in a large skillet or pot and drain off most of the fat. Mix in the chili powder, salt, and flour. Pour in the tomato juice or water. Bring to a boil, stirring as you go. Add the beans, if wanted, and simmer for 20 minutes. Serve hot in bowls. So . . . this recipe is quick, easy, and versatile. Maybe that's why it has been so popular in supermarkets.

Carroll Shelby's Original Texas Brand Chili Kit

Here's a four-packet kit that I purchase from my local Dixie Dandy store. It was formulated by Carroll Shelby, an ex-Texan good ol' boy and race car driver of Grand Prix fame. Shelby had a hand in organizing the first chili cook-offs in Terlingua and, a little later, the founding of the ICS organization in California. At one time, Shelby marketed the mix from a post office box in Los Angeles, but these days it is distributed by Reily Foods Company of Austin. Here's a recipe for quick chili, pretty much as printed on the package:

     2 pounds ground beef
     1 (8-ounce) can tomato sauce
     2 (8-ounce) cans water
     1 (4-ounce) Carroll Shelby's Chili Kit

Brown the meat in a large skillet and pour off the drippings. Mix in the tomato sauce and water. Dump in the red chili spice mix pouch from the kit, along with the packet of salt (or to taste). If you want the chili hot, stir in part or all of the small packet of powdered cayenne. Cook on low heat for 15 minutes, stirring from time to time. If you want a thicker chili, mix the contents of the masa flour pouch with ⅓ cup water and stir the paste into the pot. Simmer for

5 more minutes. Serve hot, along with shredded cheddar cheese, sour cream, or chopped tomatoes, the package says.

In addition, the kit also contains directions for making an even quicker microwave chili, and offers suggestions for making your own recipe using beans, chopped onions, bell peppers, and so on.

I won't argue with the basic recipe or the concept of the chili kit, but I wonder how much of it is really Carroll Shelby's and how much is a basic chili designed to please everybody and offend no one. I've seen other recipes attributed to Shelby that seem a little more individualist. The one published in the International Chili Society's *Official Chili Cookbook,* for instance, called for ¾ pound of grated goat cheese to be added during the cooking phase, and shredded cheddar to be used as a bowl topping. The recipe also called for both round and chuck steak, and ¼ cup ground dried Number 6 New Mexico chiles. That's being pretty specific.

Senator's Chili

Reportedly, Senator Barry Goldwater of Arizona and Senator John Tower of Texas got into a verbal shooting match in Washington, DC, each claiming his state to have the world's best chili. This resulted in a showdown cook-off, but shortly before the verdict was to be announced Tower shouted out that he was clearly the winner because his opponent had put beans into the pot. The International Chili Society, the story goes on, had final word and proclaimed Goldwater the winner. It's a good story, and the resulting commercial chili mix ain't too bad either, containing chile pepper, salt, garlic, onion, paprika, cumin, oregano, and other spices. Defiantly, the recipe not only calls for beans but specifies three kinds.

I understand that when the word of the controversy got out around Washington, some other senators recognized the attention-drawing power of chili and published their own states' versions in the Congressional Record.

I understand also that New Mexico's Senator Pete Domenici served chili to the Senate when he sponsored a bill to make chili the national dish.

> 2 pounds lean ground beef
> 1 (28-ounce) can tomato sauce or chopped tomatoes
> 1 (16-ounce) can black beans
> 1 (16-ounce) can pinto beans
> 1 (16-ounce) can kidney beans
> 1 (2.5-ounce) packet The Senator's Chili Mix
> water or beer

Brown the beef in a stovetop Dutch oven or other suitable pot. Drain the fat and add the tomato sauce or canned tomatoes, along with a can of beer or about 2 cups water. Stir in the chili mix. Bring to a simmer, reduce the heat to very low, cover tightly, and cook for ½ hour, stirring a time or two. Drain and rinse the beans, then add them to the pot. Bring to a new simmer, cover, and cook for another ½ hour, stirring and tasting several times. Makes 8 "good servings."

Note: The package of The Senator's Chili Mix contains a modified recipe to fit low-carbohydrate diets. This one omits the beans and uses ground turkey, along with the tomato sauce. During the last 10 minutes of cooking, two chopped zucchinis are added! Honest. That's what it says. What would Senator Goldwater say? What about the beer? But that's not all. The box also has a recipe for "vegetarian chili," without even the ground turkey. It calls for a bunch of your favorite vegetables (using the V-word), including zucchini and eggplant.

Note also: I have also seen a recipe attributed to Senator Tower. For 3 pounds of chili meat, it called for a 15-ounce can of tomato sauce and 2 onions along with a dozen spices and minor ingredients. No beans.

Hammett House Chili Seasoning

An address like 1616 Will Rogers (who judged a town by the quality of the chili at the local eatery) has to get attention from chiliheads. The chili seasoning is marketed in 1-quart Mason jars by Hammett House restaurant. If you want to make up your own recipe, use 1 ounce of the chili seasoning to 1 pound of meat, plus whatever else you want. Or, if you want a rather large batch of chili served Midwest style (with beans and spaghetti), here is their house recipe:

    10 pounds ground beef
    2 quarts cooked red beans
    4 pounds cooked spaghetti
    96 ounces tomato juice
    10 ounces Hammett House Chili Seasoning
    ½ cup Hammett House All-Purpose Seasoning
    diced yellow onion (for topping)
    grated cheese (for topping)
    water

Brown the beef in a stovetop Dutch oven or other suitable pot, stirring well to work all the lumps out of the meat. Drain off most of the fat. Stir in the chili and all-purpose seasonings. Add the tomato juice and enough water to cover the mixture. Cover and simmer for an hour or longer, stirring from time to time and adding more water if needed. For a three-way serving: Place cooked spaghetti on a plate and spoon chili on top. Place the beans on top of the chili. Garnish with grated cheese and diced onions. Good stuff.

Six Gun Chili Mixin's

This is one of my favorite mixes, partly because of the packaging and promotional prose. Distributed from California, it's a Texas recipe that originated near San Angelo, where selling chili was a daylight job for the founding family. (Making White Mule was the night job, discontinued now because it is illegal. What a pity. Moonshine is sometimes called for as a chili ingredient.) Anyhow, Six Gun comes in a small bag with four pouches inside: two large brown pouches of chile powder and spices, one white pouch of thickener (called masa flour), and one small red pouch of hot stuff.

2 pounds ground beef
1 (16-ounce) can tomatoes with juice
1 (16-ounce) can pinto or kidney beans (optional)
1 bag Six Gun Chili Mixin's
water as needed

Put 1 cup water into a bowl and mix in the two large brown packets. Set aside. In a large skillet, brown the ground beef and pour off most of the grease. Add the tomatoes and juice from the can. Stir the chili mixings from the bowl into the skillet. (Drain a can of pinto or kidney beans and stir them into the chili if wanted.) Bring to a boil and reduce the heat to a simmer. Now you'll have to make a decision, following the directions on the Six Gun package.

1. If you want Tenderfoot Chili (family style), wave the unopened little red pouch over the chili. Don't add any, but tell 'em you did.

2. For Outlaw Chili (medium hot), stir in half the red pepper . . . hot enough to drive in-laws out.

3. For Six Gun Chili (hot), add all the red pepper—and then stir fast if you want to keep the spoon, the firm advises.

Choose one and simmer the chili uncovered for 30 minutes or longer, adding a little water as needed. If you want a tightener, mix the contents of the white pouch with warm water and stir into the chili. Simmer a while and serve hot. Good stuff, but I add a little salt to mine and prefer to serve the beans on the side.

Hard Times Chili

This style of chili was first served, according to the promo on the package, in Cincinnati, Ohio, back in 1922, and has been a favorite at the Hard Times Cafe. Essentially, it is a chili with quite a bit of tomato sauce and paste. Beans are cooked separately and served on the side. Traditionally, Cincinnati chili is served with pasta of some sort. The spices include the usual chile powder, cumin, and oregano—along with allspice and cinnamon. The box contains two identical packets of 2 ounces each. Each packet will season 2½ pounds ground meat. The directions are a little offbeat in that the meat is not browned as usual.

2½ pounds regular-grind beef
1 (15-ounce) can tomato sauce
1 (6-ounce) can tomato paste
1 small onion, diced
1 tablespoon vinegar
1 (2-ounce) bag Hard Times spice mix
1½ cups water

Put the ground beef and water into a pot and bring to a boil. When the meat has "browned," stir in the contents of the 2-ounce spice pouch. Add the tomato sauce, tomato paste, onion, and vinegar.

Mix and simmer for ½ to 1 hour, stirring from time to time. Add a little more water if needed, bearing in mind that Cincinnati chili is traditionally served on the thin side. You now have a one-way chili, I gather.

For a two-way chili, serve with oyster crackers on the side.

For a three-way presentation, put a thin layer of spaghetti on a plate, followed by a layer of chili. Cover all with a generous sprinkling of mild shredded cheddar cheese.

For a four-way presentation, make a three-way and top the whole generously with chopped sweet onions.

A five-way? Back up. Put down the spaghetti and top with precooked red or kidney beans. Top all this with chili, cheese, and onions.

Note: I understand that the cafe is still making the chili. They also serve a Coney Dog, as discussed in chapter 17.

Big Bruce's Gunpowder Chili

This commercial mix comes in a round box with three pouches inside, enough for about 2 pounds of meat. A large package is also available for a chili party, said to season enough red to feed a herd of people. The mix is marketed by Gunpowder Foods, Inc., where Big Bruce Pinnell bills himself as the Chief Executive Pepper. Big Bruce has won a number of chili cook-offs, championships, and awards, he points out. Note that his recipe calls for two kinds of beef. The stew beef should be cut into chunks about ¾ inch thick.

1 pound lean stew beef
1 pound very lean ground beef
1 (15-ounce) can diced tomatoes or tomato sauce
1 kit Gunpowder Chili dump
1 tablespoon vegetable oil

salt to taste

water as needed

In a heavy 4-quart pot, heat the oil and brown the hamburger and stew beef, cooking for about 5 minutes. Don't drain off any fat or oil. Add 1 cup of water (more for high altitude, Big Bruce says) and the diced tomatoes. Bring to a boil, stir in spice pouch #1, cover, reduce the heat, and simmer for 1 hour with minimum stirring. (Much stirring, Big Bruce says, will break down the meat.) Relax. Have another cold sarsaparilla, he says. When the meat is almost tender, add spice pouch #2. Now is decision time. Spice pouch #3 is very hot, containing as it does habanero. Big Bruce recommends five levels of heat:

1. Well mannered = use none of the hot stuff.
2. Sassy = ½ teaspoon.
3. Rude (but socially acceptable) = 1 teaspoon.
4. Outrageous (b . . . bad to the bone) = 2 teaspoons.
5. Explosive (dial 911 first) = 3 teaspoons.

When you have made up your mind, carefully measure the spice and stir it into the pot. (Put the rest of the hot stuff into a salt-shaker for use in soups, stews, and so on, Big Bruce advises.) Simmer very slowly on very low heat for about 1 hour, or longer, depending on the toughness and size of the stew meat. Again, Big Bruce advises minimum stirring—but add water if needed and a little salt. Relax. Have another sarsaparilla as the chili simmers. Serve with corn bread—or scoop out the center of a large sourdough roll and use it as an edible bowl—along with the usual toppings, including shredded cheese, chopped onions, chopped jalapeños, and sour cream. Beans, Big Bruce says, must be cooked separately and served on the side. Also serve this chili in plates over rice or pasta.

"For best results, take your time and follow the instructions exactly. My championship spices and instructions will produce the best Bowl of Red you've ever made," Big Bruce brags.

Wick Fowler's World Championship Chili

Wick Fowler developed one of the first chili dumps and, reportedly, used it to win the 1972 World Championship, sponsored by the International Chili Society during its Texas days. Fowler had firm opinions about not cooking beans in the chili, but he did insist on a little tomato product. In any case, the recipe is refreshingly short.

2 pounds ground or diced meat
1 (8-ounce) can tomato sauce
1 package 2-Alarm chili mix (Fowler's)
2 cups water
salt to taste

Cook the meat on medium heat until it is gray. Stir in all the ingredients except for the salt and masa flour packet of the 2-Alarm mix. Cover the pot tightly and simmer for 1¼ hours, or until the meat is tender. Skim off any excess grease that floats to the top. Stir the masa flour into a little warm water, making a smooth paste. Stir the paste into the chili to thicken it. Add a little salt and simmer for another 15 minutes.

This will make a 2-Alarm chili. If you want it tamer, use only part of the red pepper pouch. For false-alarm chili, leave the pepper out entirely. For a hotter chili, simply add cayenne or other hot pepper.

Note: If you want to use such a simple recipe in a cook-off, be sure to check the regulations carefully. Chili mixes without other spice ingredients may not be allowed at some cook-offs.

Easy Home-Mixed Chili Powder

You don't necessarily have to grind dried red peppers into a powder to come up with a chili mix. The powders are available in bulk as well as in small packages from some suppliers of chili fixin's and spice products. Thus, you can easily purchase a pound of ready-ground ancho and a few ounces of the others, as, for example, for use in this recipe. It's best to get freshly ground chile powder if possible, but it will keep pretty well in sealed containers.

1 pound ancho chile powder
4 ounces mild paprika
4 ounces chile de arbol powder
4 ounces freshly ground cumin
4 ounces garlic powder
2 ounces ground oregano
1 tablespoon cayenne, or to taste

Mix all the ingredients well, put into an airtight container, and store in a cool, dark place until needed. I keep mine in the refrigerator. For making chili, use from 1 to 2 tablespoons per pound of meat. If you add lots of beans, you may want to add a little more powder. It's best, always, to add not quite enough powder early in the cooking process. Then add more as the chili develops, stirring and tasting from time to time.

CHILI DEVIATIONS AND WAYWARD TRENDS

One modern book on chili allows the cook to add pretty much what he chooses. If a can or two of potted meat or a dash or two of A1 seem to be missing, feel free to add them, the philosophy goes. I'll have to admit that he-man chili with proper amounts of red meat, chile pulp, and cumin will take a lot of abuse. In a big pot of hearty red, a few crushed fenugreek seeds won't hurt a thing. Oh, I might hee-haw a little about the prunes and crème fraîche, but I won't refuse a bowl or two of the chili for eating purposes.

What I really do object to, as I pointed out in the introduction, is what is being left out of our modern chili. And the omission is sometimes not too apparent—especially if the list of ingredients is as long as your leg. Consider the following examples.

A recipe billed as jerk chili contains only ¼ teaspoon of chili powder and no additional cumin. It also contains some jerk seasoning, which, in turn, is distinguished by a really hot pepper of the habanero family, allspice (a Jamaican native), and other spices. But the total chile pepper is minuscule. The result is a really hot Jamaican stew, but it's not chili. Not really.

Other examples include a recipe for filé chili. It calls for quite a few ingredients, as many Cajun and Creole dishes do these days. Its 3 pounds of meat and various vegetables make a sizable batch. The lead-in to the recipe says the filé adds a subtle taste. Well, filé is used mostly as a thickener for gumbo and other stews. As for taste, a mere ⅓ teaspoon in a large pot of chili won't stand up to 6 teaspoons cumin powder, although some Cajuns will want to argue the matter.

More to the point, the filé chili recipe does not contain any chili powder or chile powder, except for a scant ¼ teaspoon cayenne. It does call for 1 green bell pepper and 3 jalapeño peppers, neither of which will add any red to the pot. The almost complete absence of dried red pepper (except for the pinch of cayenne) really takes the "chile" out of the stew.

In *How to Cook Everything,* one of the better basic cookbooks for these times, Mark Bittman gives us some excellent information on beans and how to cook them. The main recipe for chili, however, leaves a lot to be desired, at least for me. It contains no meat and not much chile. Indeed, one could well cook the recipe without any chile at all, owing to the way the optional ingredients are handled in the recipe. (The ingredients list calls for 1 fresh or dried chile, listed as optional. It also calls for 1 tablespoon chili powder, also listed as optional. Eliminate both options and you've got no chile left.) Thus, we could end up with a dish that contains no carne and no chile whatsoever. Yet, the title of the recipe is Chili con Carne! Well, it's merely a bean dish. (Under this main recipe, I must add to be fair, Bittman adds two variations, one with tomatoes and one with meat—1 pound of chopped or ground beef, pork, turkey, or chicken.)

In another example, a big-batch chile recipe in *Le Cookbook,* published in Paris and billed as U.S.O. Chili con Carne, called for 10 tablespoons of chili powder—*or* 4 tablespoons powdered oregano, 4 tablespoons powdered garlic, 2 tablespoons caraway seeds, and ½ teaspoon cayenne. The substitution eliminates almost all of the chile in the recipe (except for ½ teaspoon cayenne)—and entirely does in the cumin! Clearly, the French don't understand chile, but ignorance is not an acceptable excuse.

5

CHILI WITH BEANS AND EXTENDERS

Once chili became established as a quick, easy, and inexpensive way to feed soldiers, wayfarers, cowboys, peasant folk, bread-liners, and others, it was natural to add beans, rice, and pasta to increase the bulk while decreasing the price. Beans were a natural extender, probably used, along with the tomato, by at least some of the original Indians. In time some people came to regard beans as an essential ingredient in chili. They are still standard in most American recipes, although abstainers are quite adamant.

The way to appease both camps, I maintain, is to cook the beans separately and add them as wanted to individual servings. That should satisfy most people. But it won't. And even after you agree on how the beans are to be cooked and served, the question of which bean to use will surely arise. Some allow only pinto beans. Others insist on red kidney beans. Still others will want a mix of several kinds.

Pretty much the same statement can be said about cooking rice and pasta with chili, except that the numbers are smaller on both sides. Some will want regular white rice while others hold out for brown, and a few will surprise us with Himalayan red. And chili with pasta can include old favorites ranging from elbow macaroni and spaghetti to the tiny orzo and the wide zitoni. Suit yourself, al dente or otherwise.

BEANS

Probably the most popular bean used in chili is the pinto, with red kidney beans coming in second. There are regional favorites, too, and some recipes call for three or more kinds of beans or legumes, including black-eyed peas, butterbeans, and so on.

By far most of the beans used in American chili are canned. Because canned beans are already on the soft side, I feel that they should not be put into the chili pot during the cooking phase, or should be held out until the last few minutes of cooking. Some bean enthusiasts, however, will want them put into the pot at the outset. Some will want the beans mushy—even mashed. An old army recipe, for example, calls for almost a gallon of beans. Two-thirds of these are ground in a meat chopper before stirring into the pot, and the others are put in whole.

Note that beans can also be cooked separately and served as a side dish or a topping. These go-withs are covered in chapter 18. Here are a few recipes calling for beans as ingredient.

Chili with Dry Pinto Beans

Do not soak the beans for this recipe. If you do, they will become mushy during the long cooking period.

> 2 pounds diced beef (about ½ inch)
> 1 cup dry pinto beans
> 2 large tomatoes, chopped
> 2 medium-to-large onions, chopped
> 4 toes garlic, minced
> 4 tablespoons ancho chile powder
> 1 tablespoon peanut oil

1 tablespoon freshly ground cumin seeds
½ tablespoon Mexican oregano
cracker meal as needed
water as needed
salt to taste
red pepper flakes to taste

Heat the peanut oil in a suitable pot or Dutch oven. Sauté the meat until it is gray, stirring as you go and slowly mixing in the ancho powder, oregano, and cumin. Add the onion and garlic. Cook until the onion is clear. Rinse the pinto beans in a bowl of water, throwing out any that float along with any foreign matter. Add the pinto beans, tomatoes, salt, and red pepper flakes to the pot along with enough water to cover the ingredients by about 1 inch. Bring to a light boil, quickly reduce the heat to very low, cover tightly, and simmer for about 4 hours. It is important to add water and stir from time to time, remembering that the pinto beans will expand and soak up water as they cook. About 30 minutes before time to eat, stir in a little cracker meal to thicken the gravy to your liking. Serve hot in bowls, along with crackers and suitable go-withs.

Tampa Bay Three-Bean Chili

Here's a recipe that calls for garbanzo beans, which is what chickpeas have been called in parts of Florida for many years owing to the Cuban influence in the old Tampa cigar district. This particular recipe calls for only a small amount of chili powder and no extra cumin; so, adjust the seasoning during the tasting phase if necessary to suit your taste.

1 pound ground round
1 pound highly seasoned country sausage

10 slices bacon
1 (16-ounce) can garbanzo beans
1 (16-ounce) can pinto beans
1 (16-ounce) can kidney beans
6 cups chopped tomatoes
1 large Spanish onion, chopped
1 red bell pepper, seeded and chopped
4 cloves garlic, minced
1 hot chile pepper, seeded and minced (try a Florida datil, if
    you have one)
1 cup red wine
½ cup Worcestershire sauce
2 teaspoons chili powder (or more to taste)
2 teaspoons dry mustard
2 teaspoons celery seeds
salt and freshly ground black pepper to taste
cumin to taste (optional)

Brown the bacon in a stovetop Dutch oven. Drain and set aside. Brown the beef in the bacon drippings. Drain and set aside. Cut the sausage into wheels, brown, drain, and set aside. Pour off most of the drippings left in the pot, leaving about 1 tablespoon. Sauté the onion, bell pepper, chile pepper, and garlic for 3 or 4 minutes, stirring as you go with a wooden spoon. Add the chili powder and other spices. Stir in the wine and Worcestershire sauce. Add the tomatoes and simmer for 10 minutes. Add the beef, sausage wheels, and crumbled bacon. Bring to a boil, reduce the heat to very low, cover, and simmer for at least 30 minutes. Stir in the beans, along with the liquid from the cans, and bring to a new boil. Reduce the heat, cover, and simmer for an hour, stirring from time to time and adding a little water if needed. Serve hot with crackers on the side.

Note: The garbanzo beans add a certain crunch to this chili. If you like the sensation, try the next recipe, made with dry beans instead of canned.

A. D.'s Garbanzo Bean Chili

Garbanzo beans don't have much flavor but they do have a firm texture that does wonders for soups and stews. Moreover, they hold up to long, slow cooking, making them ideal for chili. Even the leftovers have crunch. By comparison, most other beans tend to become mushy if overcooked. Although colored varieties are available, garbanzo beans are normally cream colored, making them stand out unforgettably in a bowl of red. Dry garbanzos are available in supermarkets under the name chickpeas or garbanzos, and sometimes both names are available in different sections of the store. The authors of most modern recipes calling for chorizo insist on peeling them before cooking. I don't bother, but suit yourself.

2 pounds ground beef
½ pound chorizo or spicy country sausage
12 ounces dry garbanzo beans
1 medium-to-large onion, chopped
⅓–½ cup ancho or New Mexico chile powder
1–2 teaspoons cumin seeds
salt and black pepper to taste
hot water

Cut the sausage into ½- to ¾-inch wheels. Brown the ground beef, sausage, and onion in a large stovetop Dutch oven or other suitable pot. Cover with hot water and bring to a boil. While the water heats, toast the cumin seeds lightly in a small skillet. When the pot boils, sprinkle in most of the chile powder and cumin. Rinse the garbanzo beans and add to the pot. Bring to a new boil, reduce the heat, cover tightly, and simmer for an hour, stirring from time to time and adding more water as needed. (The garbanzo beans soak up some of the liquid, so watch the pot carefully.) Stir in the salt and black pepper to taste. Simmer for an hour. Taste and add more chile powder or cumin if needed. Cover and simmer for another hour or two. Serve hot in bowls with rolled cornmeal tortillas on the side.

Chili with Soy

Although more and more soy products such as tofu are being used in American cookery, especially among the health food set, the beans themselves are seldom listed in recipes. Yet, they are edible either fresh or dried, and, of course, they are raised in great tonnage in this country. Even so, most of our farmers and their wives have never cooked a single soybean. In any case, here's an old recipe adapted from The Progressive Farmer's Southern Cookbook, *which says the chili can be cooked with chopped lean pork or chicken as well as beef.*

1 pound finely chopped lean beef
2 cups chopped tomatoes
1 cup dry soybeans
¼ cup butter (divided)
1 onion, finely sliced
1 tablespoon chili powder
1 teaspoon salt
½ teaspoon black pepper

Soak the soybeans overnight. The next morning, drain the beans, put them into a suitable pot, cover with water, and cook until they are tender. While waiting, brown the onion in 2 tablespoons of the butter in a skillet. Put the onion into the pot with the beans. Brown the beef in the remaining butter, cooking and stirring for about 5 minutes. Add the tomatoes, chili powder, salt, and black pepper. Add the contents of the skillet to the beans in the pot. Bring to a boil, reduce the heat to very low, cover tightly, and simmer for 20 minutes or longer before serving. Feeds 2 to 4.

Chili El Cajun

The Cajuns get carried away with spices and other ingredients added to the simplest of recipes, and often they refer to other recipes requiring even more ingredients. Anytime you can find a Cajun recipe with only 22 ingredients, all in one block, you're in luck. The unusual ingredient in this one, adapted from the book Cajun Men Cook, *is a large batch of refried beans instead of regular beans. The refried beans make for an interesting texture, making the recipe more filling without the beans being visible. The recipe calls for either ground beef or ground turkey. I'll take the beef, but any good meat can be used. Try ground rabbit or Louisiana nutria, if available.*

> 3 pounds ground chuck or turkey
> 3 (16-ounce) cans refried beans
> 1 (10¾-ounce) can chicken noodle soup
> 1 (10¾-ounce) can chicken broth
> 2 (8-ounce) cans tomato sauce
> ¼ cup olive oil
> ¼ cup dry sherry
> 2 large onions, chopped
> 3 ribs celery, chopped with part of green tops
> 1 large bell pepper, chopped

2 tablespoons fresh parsley, chopped
2 ounces chili powder
1 tablespoon cumin, freshly ground
1 tablespoon oregano (optional)
1 tablespoon paprika
1 tablespoon dehydrated chicken bouillon
1 tablespoon sugar
1 tablespoon salt
1 teaspoon freshly ground black pepper
1 teaspoon granulated garlic
1 teaspoon baking soda
pinch red pepper (cayenne)
water (if needed)
cornstarch (if needed)

Heat the oil in a large stovetop Dutch oven and brown the meat. Add the onions, celery, and bell pepper. Cook for 5 or 6 minutes, stirring a time or two with a wooden spoon, until the onions are tender. Gradually stir in the rest of the ingredients according to size (as listed above)—all except the baking soda, water, and cornstarch. Bring almost to a boil, then cover and simmer on very low heat for at least an hour, stirring a time or two. When ready to serve, stir in the baking soda and cook for another 10 minutes, or until the bubbles stop coming. Taste for seasonings, perhaps adding pepper, cayenne, or salt, as needed. If the chili is too thick to suit you, dilute with a little water. If too thin, thicken with cornstarch mixed with water (mix 2 tablespoons cornstarch in ½ cup of water, shake or stir, and use as needed). Serve hot in bowls. The Cajuns say it goes well with potato salad or coleslaw, served with Mexican corn bread and perhaps topped with grated cheddar cheese.

Note: I haven't done a survey, but a lot of Cajun chili recipes seem to include quite a bit of chopped onion, bell pepper, and celery—sometimes called the Trinity of Cajun or Creole cooking. Sometimes these ingredients are stirred into the chili at the end, without much cooking, or used as a topping.

Betty Ford's Chili with Beans

A recipe attributed to Betty Ford, adapted here from the Official Chili Cookbook, *calls for beans that have been soaked overnight. They are then cooked separately, with a little chili powder, and added to the chili pot at the last minute. Interesting. And it's a short, sensible recipe, although I would prefer to reduce the bean measure by half.*

1 ½ pounds ground round
1 pound dried red beans
2 medium onions, chopped
4 tablespoons chili powder (divided)
3 tablespoons shortening
salt to taste

Rinse the red beans, cover with plain water, and soak overnight. Drain, put into a pot with unsalted water, and cook, covered, on low heat until soft. Add 2 tablespoons of the chili powder and a little salt. Set the pot aside. In a skillet, heat the shortening and sauté the onions until soft. Add the ground round, the rest of the chili powder, and salt. Cook until the meat is lightly browned, stirring as you go. Add enough water to cover, reduce the heat, and simmer for 20 minutes or longer. Add the meat to the bean pot, stir in, cook for a few minutes, and serve hot. Feeds 4 to 6.

Chili with Lentils or Quick-Cook Beans

Lentils cook in about 20 minutes, making them a good choice for a quick chili.

  2 pounds ground chuck
  6 ounces dried lentils
  1 (8-ounce) can tomato sauce
  1 medium onion, chopped
  4 cloves garlic, minced
  4 tablespoons chili powder
  1 teaspoon ground cumin
  salt and cayenne to taste

Sauté the ground chuck in a large skillet, stirring until the meat has turned gray and all the lumps have been broken up. Add the chopped onion and garlic. Cook for another 4 or 5 minutes, stirring a time or two. Stir in the chili powder, cumin, salt, and cayenne. Add the tomato sauce and lentils, along with enough water to cover by at least 1 inch. Cook on low heat for 25 minutes, stirring a time or two and adding more water if needed. Serve hot in bowls.

Note: Some other beans cook in a relatively short time, and some of these, such as Jacob's cattle, are quite pretty. So, use whatever kind of bean you want instead of the lentils in this recipe, adjusting the simmering time as required for each kind of bean. Remember that the beans will expand and soak up lots of water. So, watch the pot.

CHILI WITH PASTA, RICE, AND WHOLE GRAINS

Although rice and pasta make excellent go-withs or optional toppings, in some regions they are considered essential ingredients to the chili recipe. In general, any kind of uncooked rice or pasta can be added to the pot during the last 25 to 30 minutes of cooking. Just make sure that you have plenty of liquid in the pot—and plenty of room—remembering that most grains will absorb liquid and expand as they cook.

Using pasta, such as macaroni and spaghetti, in chili is pretty much a manner of serving, as discussed under "Midwestern Chili" in chapter 16. For this reason, I am not offering a recipe in this chapter. It is easy, however, to add a little pasta to the pot during the cooking phase.

The same can be said of rice, and it is more widely used as an ingredient, not a go-with. A recipe is included below. True rice devotees will probably want to use brown rice as an ingredient.

Other grains can also be used as extenders in chili, including wheat berries and barley. Put them into the pot at the outset and make sure they are cooked soft before serving the chili (unless you have some sort of quick-cook grain). I don't recommend using whole grains in chili from a culinary point of view, but as a practical matter they can serve a useful purpose, adding nutritional value at modest cost. I am including a recipe below for barley, which is often considered a soup ingredient, but in general the cook should become familiar with the dozens of grains that can be used—especially their cooking times. Quinoa, for example, tends to become mushy if cooked too long, whereas whole wheat berries can be cooked half a day.

Mess Kit Chili

This old army recipe came from a War Department document published in 1896. It was designed for the individual soldier to cook with the aid of a mess kit. It's also an ideal recipe for cooking in a camp skillet, perhaps using venison instead of beefsteak. The measures can be increased as needed, if you have a full kitchen or a big camp pot. The original did not call for cumin, but I have added it as an optional ingredient for modern partakers.

1 round beefsteak
2 tablespoons rice
2 large dried red chile pods
1 tablespoon bacon drippings or cooking oil
dried onion flakes
flour
salt
½ teaspoon ground cumin
boiling water

Cut the steak into a ½-inch dice. Cook for a few minutes in the bacon drippings, then stir in a cup of hot water, dried onion flakes, salt, cumin, and the rice. Cook until the meat is very tender, stirring from time to time and adding more water if needed. While waiting for the meat to cook (or perhaps before you even start cooking the meat), seed and devein the peppers. Soak them for a while in a cup of boiling water. Steep until cool. Then—check this—squeeze the peppers in the hand until the water is thick and red. Add a little flour if needed to thicken. Set aside. When the meat is very tender, stir in the chile sauce and serve hot.

A. D.'s Pearl Barley Chili with Barley Beer

Barley in one form or another has always been a popular soup ingredient, and it works well as an extender in chili. Hulled barley (available in some health food stores) is best because it must be cooked for a long time, making it ideal for a chili that is to be simmered all day. These days, however, pearl barley (which is polished, removing part of the grain) is more common and is available in most supermarkets, often in the soup section. If you use any kind of quick-cook barley, which I don't recommend, remember that it should be added to the pot toward the end of the cooking period, following the instructions on the package.

> 2 pounds lean beef, cut into ¾-inch cubes
> ½ cup pearl barley
> 2 ounces salt pork
> ¼ cup minced onion
> 2 cloves garlic, minced
> 4 tablespoons pure chile powder (ancho or New Mexico)
> 1 tablespoon freshly ground cumin seeds
> ¼ teaspoon dried Mexican oregano
> salt and freshly ground black pepper to taste
> canned beef stock
> beer as needed (a barley product)

Cook the salt pork in a large skillet until the pieces give up most of their fat and are crispy. Drain the cracklings and set aside. Brown the beef in the pork fat. Add the barley and enough stock to barely cover. Then pour in about an inch of beer. Stir in the onion and garlic. Sprinkle on the chile powder, cumin, oregano, salt, and freshly ground black pepper. Heat to a light boil, then reduce the heat and simmer for 2 or 3 hours, uncovered—or longer if you are lucky enough to have hulled barley instead of pearl. Stir and taste from time to time with a wooden spoon, adding beef stock (or beer) as needed. Toward the end, cook down until the chili is quite thick. Serve hot in bowls, topping each serving off with a dollop of sour cream and a sprinkling of the reserved cracklings. Good stuff.

6

OTHER CHILI INGREDIENTS— FOR BETTER OR WORSE

Not all the topics in this chapter include recipes. Nor should they. Take mesquite blossoms, for example, as an ingredient for chili. Anyone who has some at hand and wants to try them in chili can simply put them into the pot. Hell, they put everything else in— and that's the point, really.

On the serious side, this chapter is not limited to whimsical ingredients. It does contain some useful information on important topics, such as thinners and thickeners, and tips or opinions on how to use them. Most of the comments under these topics can be applied to a number of recipes for chili, as well as to soups and stews in general. Hence, the entry should exist on its own—often in fussy detail—for possible application in a number of recipes.

THINNERS

Liquids of one sort or another are usually added to a pot of chili to provide flavor and moisture. The flavor may or may not be needed, but the additional moisture is essential, especially for chili cooked the right way: long and slow over low heat. Many jackleg cooks insist on putting beer into their chili, and some recipes even call for wine. These are covered below, with the recommended dosage for ardent spirits listed under whiskey. Beverages for drinking with a bowl of chili are covered under a separate heading at the end of chapter 18.

Water. By far the most useful thinner used in chili is plain water. Of course, the water evaporates and has to be replaced to keep the bottom of the chili from scorching. Ordinary tap water will do if it's fit to drink, but some cooks will prefer to use bottled mineral water. Note that the amount of water to be used in making chili will vary, depending on the length of cooking time, the heat, and how tightly the pot lid fits.

As a rule, the liquid—often water combined with other liquids such as tomato juice—should barely cover the meat when the cooking begins. Be careful, however, when cooking dry beans or rice in a pot of chili. These will swell considerably, soaking up lots of liquid.

Meat Stocks. Meat stocks are often listed in the ingredients list for chili recipes. These add flavor and body to chili and are especially useful in recipes that call for a small amount of meat with lots of beans and tomatoes. At one time, meat stocks were commonly prepared in the home kitchen, but the trend these days is to buy canned stocks and broths at the supermarket. Homemade stock is better if the cook has some good soup bones to work with, but canned stock will do, and a cup or two of water with bouillon cubes will do in a pinch.

Coffee. The practice of using coffee in redeye gravy as an ingredient in some stews no doubt goes back to the time when running water wasn't available in the kitchen or on the chuck wagon. The cook simply used what was at hand—including coffee left over from breakfast. In any case, black coffee makes an interesting thinner for chili, especially when it has been brewed from freshly ground beans. Use it sparingly, however.

Beer. This is by far the most popular alcoholic addition to chili, especially to large pots that simmer for a long time while good ol' boys stand around talking, tasting, and sipping from time to time. Often a pot of chili made with beer might be the best ever made—but the cook may have lost track of exactly what's in it. Any good American beer will do for chili, but these days many cooks, especially in Texas and the Southwest, will specify Mexican beer. How much? I think half a can with 2 pounds of meat will do. Then drink off the rest.

Soda Pop. Some people like Coca-Cola (Classic, of course) in their chili. Others want Pepsi. Even 7UP.

Wine. I'll allow a little dry red wine in my chili, about ½ cup per 2 pounds of meat, but really good burgundy ought to be reserved for a table wine served with steak au poivre by candlelight. Somehow, wine and the taste of cumin, which seems to be necessary for modern chili, just don't jibe. And, of course, putting white wine in chili would be uncivilized.

Tequila. Distilled cactus juice has become a popular cocktail ingredient in the United States, inspiring such drinks as the bloody Maria and margarita, and it seems to work better in chili than gin or vodka. I've even seen one recipe called Margarita Chili, with tequila and lime juice in the ingredients, that is served in a bowl rimmed with salt, margarita style!

Other ardent cactus juices such as pulque and mezcal can also be used in chili, along with the worm in the bottle if you are feeding culinary sports.

Whiskey. Bibulous champions and their arguments aside, any good whiskey—Tennessee sour mash, Kentucky bourbon, Canadian blended—will do for adding to a pot of chili. Just pour with a steady hand and don't overdo it. Allow no more than 2 ounces of whiskey for each 2 pounds of meat in the recipe.

Whisky. Spelled without an e, Scotch whisky is a passion with some chefs and jackleg cooks. Some of these people will put even expensive single-malt Scotch into a pot of red. Although I think it is a waste of good booze, I can't argue with the results if used in moderation. In *The Great Chili Book,* Bill Bridges tells about a man from Florida (one Stuart Cumming) going to a good ol' boy chili cook-off down in Terlingua, Texas, and putting Scotch into his pot of bubbling chili while—picture this—wearing a kilt.

THICKENERS AND TIGHTENERS

A good many ingredients are commonly used to thicken a bowl of red—but remember that chile made with plenty of mild chile pepper pulp cooks down with a nice texture and really needs no thickening if not much water or other liquid is added. Still, many people will want to proceed with a rather thin chili, then thicken it at the end of the cooking period with flour, fine cornmeal, and so on. A few recipes refer to these ingredients as tighteners. Often these ingredients are merely stirred into the chili in powdered form during the last 10 minutes of cooking, or they can be dissolved in a little water before being added to the pot as a paste.

The ingredients below add a little nutrition and bulk to chili, but in the main they are used as thickening agents.

Wheat Flour. Ordinary white flour is often used to thicken gravies and stews and works nicely in chili. Some recipes call for flour, often stirred in toward the end of the cooking period, and some commercial mixes and dumps include flour in the ingredients. It's usually easier to mix the flour with a little water, making a paste, to be stirred in as needed. Whole wheat flour can also be used in most recipes.

Cornmeal. Many recipes call for masa harina, and the stuff is also an ingredient in many of the chili mixes and dumps. Although it will do the job and has a long shelf life, being highly processed, it has lost the good earthy flavor of corn. Most brand-name supermarket cornmeals, usually yellow, are also tasteless and often gritty in texture. Both masa harina and commercial cornmeal will work nicely as thickening agents, but freshly ground whole-kernel corn, sometimes called stone-ground or water-ground meal, is much better. In earlier texts it was sometimes called Indian meal. If you've got the right stuff, use it in any chili recipe that calls for cornmeal or masa harina—and use it to replace the dump pouches in chili mixes.

Breadstuffs. A number of fresh and stale breads can be used to thicken chili, usually crumbled or crushed. Cracker crumbs are convenient to use, and make a good tightener. Corn bread as well as biscuits and other breadstuffs can be crumbled into a bowl of red to thicken it during the cooking process, often toward the end.

Other Thickeners. A wide number of starches can be used to thicken chili, and some of these, such as kudzu, made from the huge bulb that grows on the high climbing vine that has covered parts of the South, can be used as attention-getting "secret" ingredients. Ground seeds and nuts also make good thickeners, as the Native Americans knew. These include mesquite bean meal (now touted as a miracle health food), ground sunflower seeds, and sweet chestnut flour. Peanut butter is also used as a tightener and is, in fact, used in many parts of the world as a cooking ingredient.

Spoon Coatings

It's hard to have greasy-spoon-type chili without some animal fat or some sort of vegetable oil or shortening. Some people hold that the fat is essential to a good bowl of red, providing taste, texture, and fuel for warding off a cold day. Fat also helps prevent the chili from scorching on the bottom during long simmering.

These days people are likely to consider fat to be a toxic substance, believing that fat begets fat. I hold that dry meats profit, culinarily speaking, from a little seasoning. But there are limits to the amount of fat that most Americans, except possibly the Eskimo, can safely consume. My advice to anyone in good health is to cut back on the hamburgers and french fries, both of which contain fat-making carbohydrates as well as grease and oil, and to follow your inclination when making chili and frying fish. In other words, use fats and oil in moderation and bide your time. Sooner or later, like a good three-button jacket, cooking with fat will become socially acceptable, politically correct, and maybe even nutritionally desirable. (If not, the next heading sets forth some tips for avoiding fat in chili.)

Before proceeding with a few favorite cooking fats, here are a few other topics to consider.

Some chiliheads, especially Texans, insist that fat gives a bowl of chili character as well as flavor and nutrition. Astute students of chili made with lots of chile pulp will be familiar with a strange red oil that forms on top of a pot of chili, usually visible in streaks. I think this comes from the chile peppers, and I consider it to be the mark of a superior bowl of red. A few culinary sports skim this oil off and save it for making sauces, but, personally, I like to stir it into the pot of chili before it is ladled into bowls—or use it in a dumpling recipe.

In any case, here are some of the fats and oil that we sometimes see in chili recipes, usually added to the pot to help brown the meat and onions. The grease keeps the meat from sticking to the bottom of the pot and in general helps in the browning process. If you don't want the grease, try sprinkling the bottom of the skillet or pot with coarse salt, which will also help prevent sticking. If you don't want either the grease or the salt, simply braise the meat in a little water.

Meat Fat, Bacon Drippings, and Salt Pork. Drippings from smoked bacon or salt pork are great for browning chili meat, if you don't mind the animal fat for reasons of health. Also, any fat trimmed from the meat before grinding it can be rendered and used for browning.

Suet and Tallow. Following the publication of an old recipe that called for beef suet, a doctor in Tallahassee, Florida, once wrote me at some length, claiming, in short, that the stuff is pure poison. He may be right, but some of the best cooks insist it is the best medium in which to fry a steak. Suet is simply animal fat (usually beef and sometimes sheep) taken from around the kidneys and loins. It's a firm white fat, sometimes called sweet suet. At one time suet was available in meat shops, but these days it is not generally displayed. Talk to your butcher.

Other kinds of beef fat, such as trimmings from T-bone steaks, can be tried out (fried) and used as suet. A few recipes call for beef tallow. Sometimes called taller, this is simply the comparatively hard fat from around the muscles.

Lard. At one time, lard was widely available in all grocery stores, often being packaged in a 5-gallon tin called a lard can. It's still available, but is usually refrigerated instead of being put on the shelf with a dozen cooking oils. Lard was once very important to the home cook, and that may be the reason behind the practice of fattening hogs before the slaughter. At hog killing time, the fat was cut into small chunks, dried out in large iron pots, and put into lard cans. What's left of the chunks of fat was called cracklings (which too many modern writers confused somehow with pork skin). Lard has a long shelf life, especially if stored in a dark, cool place. In addition to providing cooking fat for the winter, lard was also used to preserve cooked sausage patties. Purists will know that all lard is not on equal footing, culinarily speaking, with the best coming from the leaf fat around the kidneys.

Other Animal Fat. Contrary to popular opinion, the fat from chickens, ducks, and geese make excellent cooking oils, and some wild animals—especially bear—were once highly prized as a source of oil.

Vegetable Oil. These days we have dozens of kinds of cooking oils made from plants, nuts, or seeds. I often use peanut oil, partly because I was raised on a peanut farm and partly because it has a high smoke point. Any of the market oils will do for chili, usually used to brown the meat at the start of the cooking process. Olive oil is currently in vogue and will do just fine. Canola oil, a clever marketing term for the old rapeseed oil, is also popular. Be careful with sesame seed oil. The Asian kind, usually marketed in the foreign foods section, usually in small bottles, has been made with toasted sesame seeds and has a strong flavor. The sesame oil usually marketed in the cooking oil section will be mild and tasteless.

Vegetable Shortening. This soft, solid fat is made from vegetable oil, usually soybean oil and cottonseed oil. Although it can be used for browning meat for chili, it holds no advantage over vegetable oil and may not be as healthy. It is changed chemically by converting the polyunsaturated properties of liquid oil to the dread saturated fat of the solid form . . . or something like that.

Bone Marrow. The best seasoning for a bowl of chili comes from bone marrow, a tasty animal fat. In Alaska, caribou bone marrow is called Eskimo butter. If the marrow and the meat come from the same cut, such as beef shanks, so much the better.

Butter and Margarine. A few years ago, it was widely reported in newspapers and magazines, and on television, that margarine was better for your health than butter. Now—after many old recipes have been changed to read "margarine" instead of "butter"—the thinking has been reversed, at least in some quarters. Will it change back? In any case, I'll stick with butter simply because it tastes better. These days ordinary "butter" is being changed to read "unsalted butter." Suit yourself, but I say that a little salt improves the flavor and makes the butter much easier to store.

Getting the Fat Out

Although some people of the old school (and I am one) fully believe that a certain amount of animal fat is essential for a good bowl of red, modern health-conscious folks may want to reduce it, sometimes on doctor's orders.

Often the fat is added to a skillet or pot to help brown the meat, in which case much of it can be drained off before proceeding. Browning the meat in olive oil instead of animal fat will help, or at least be friendlier to those concerned about fat. Remember also that oil or fat isn't really needed to "brown" the meat. The real purpose of this operation is not to color the meat but instead to break ground meat up so that you won't have chunks in the chili. The oil helps keep the bottom of the meat from burning. A little water will serve the same purpose.

Chili made from market-ground beef is likely to have lots of fat. It's best to brown the beef in a skillet or suitable pot, then pour off some of the excess drippings before adding other ingredients. Using lean meat will also help. (In supermarket ground meats, ground round is much lower in fat than the ground chuck or the regular market grind.) Bison, venison, ostrich, and some other good red meats are leaner than beef, and these are becoming more widely available these days.

A few people try to skim the fat off the surface of the chili. Others sprinkle oatmeal or crumbled crackers on top of the pot of chili; when it soaks up the grease, it is skimmed off and discarded.

Anyone who is really serious about removing the fat ought to cook the chili a day ahead, making it rather soupy. Chill it overnight by setting the whole pot into the refrigerator. Almost all of the fat will rise to the surface and harden, and can be chipped off and removed with a fork or spoon. Then reheat the chili and serve.

A. D.'s Two-Day Low-Fat Chili

I have designed this recipe mainly to illustrate the several ways of removing the fat in a bowl of red, it that's what the doctor orders, while at the same time leaving in the flavor. The list below contains a minimum of ingredients, but the technique can be easily adapted to longer recipes.

2 pounds ground red meat
3 tablespoons chili powder
salt and freshly ground black pepper
other spices as needed
water as needed

Heat about ¼ cup water in a small pot with a tight-fitting lid. Add the meat and stir until it breaks apart and loses its red color. Simmer for about 15 minutes. Pour off all the surplus liquid (which will contain some fat). Cover the meat with hot water and add the chili powder, salt, pepper, and other spices if wanted. Stir well, cover, and simmer for half an hour or longer, stirring from time to time and adding more water if needed to make a rather thin gravy. Remove the pot or skillet from the heat and let it cool to room temperature. Then put the whole works into the refrigerator. Leave overnight or longer, up to 2 days. Remove the pot and, using a fork or spoon, chip off any white solid from the top. This solid will contain almost all the fat. Throw it out and reheat the pot, simmering now until you thicken the chili to your liking. Adjust the seasonings if needed. Serve hot with low-fat go-withs.

TOMATOES AND TOMATO PRODUCTS

In one form or another, tomatoes are popular in chili, although some Texans won't allow even a tablespoon of tomato sauce. Fresh tomatoes are sometimes used, but usually it's easier to dump the contents of a few cans into the pot, including whole tomatoes, chopped tomatoes, pureed tomatoes, stewed tomatoes, and seasoned tomatoes such as Italian tomatoes and Rotel, a mix of tomatoes and chili peppers. (I once looked at a so-called Native American chili recipe that called for canned tomatoes with basil!) Related products include catsup, tomato soup, tomato sauce, tomato paste, and tomato-based salsa. An Alaskan recipe instructs us to use at least two forms of tomatoes in chili—and recommends three kinds: tomato puree or canned tomatoes cut into dice, tomato paste, and tomato sauce. If you use several kinds of tomato, especially at a chili cook-off, it is customary to squash them all together with your hands.

Some people pour copious amounts of catsup on or into anything they eat, and I have seen rednecks who use the stuff as an extender for a bowl of chili, especially if the price covers all the crackers one can eat. A few other people use catsup as a major ingredient in recipes. In fact, while working on this book, I purchased a bowl of chili at a senior citizens fund-raising event. It seemed to contain only ground beef, canned beans, and catsup. No chile peppers. No cumin. It was the worst "chili" I have ever encountered.

Fresh tomatoes can be used in a recipe instead of canned ones, remembering that 1½ to 2 cups will approximate a 16-ounce can. A few persnickety cooks insist on peeling and seeding the tomatoes. I don't think peeling is necessary, especially if the chili is to be simmered for a long period of time. But suit yourself.

Green tomatoes are rarely used in chili, but there are exceptions, such as the recipe for Garlic Chili in chapter 7.

CORN AND CORN PRODUCTS

Many people are surprised to learn that cornmeal is called for in some chili recipes. Usually it is considered a thickener, as discussed earlier in this chapter. Here are a couple of other surprises that work as true ingredients.

Hominy. This old staple is dried corn that has been soaked in a lye solution, often with the lye leached from hardwood (preferably oak) ashes. The corn is soaked in the solution for several days, which softens the tough outer husk. As the kernel soaks up water and expands, the husks pop off and can be easily removed. The name "hominy" comes from a Native American term meaning "skinless corn."

Both white and yellow canned hominy can be purchased in most large supermarkets from Florida to Alaska. The canned will do just fine if used as a go-with for chili, or an ingredient added during the last half hour of the cooking phase.

Dried hominy, sometimes called posole, can be purchased from some southwestern and specialized markets. It is available in white, yellow, blue, and red. Dried hominy is quite hard and should be cooked until it is soft. I add it to chili early during the cooking. Note that dried hominy will expand like beans or rice, so be sure to keep plenty of liquid in the pot.

Some people confuse hominy and grits. They are separate corn products, and the term "hominy grits" is misleading. I don't want to get deeply into the argument here, but I'll add that grits aren't normally served with chili. I wouldn't be surprised, however, to see a recipe calling for polenta, as Italian grits are called.

Chicos. This unusual product is made from fresh corn cut from the cob in whole-kernel form and then dried. (Hominy, by comparison, is made from mature corn dried in the field.) Chicos makes an interesting addition to a bowl of red, added at the beginning of the cooking stage. It is available in dried form in some markets that specialize in southwestern cuisine. It's very good stuff.

ONIONS AND GARLIC

Onions are great additions to chili, especially if they are diced and browned in bacon drippings early in the cooking. Any good onion will do for cooking, and the medium-sized brown or white onions packed in net bags at the supermarket are suitable.

Minced garlic is a great chili ingredient, and some people consider garlic in one form or another to be essential to a proper bowl of red. It is available year-round in dried form, but gardeners can also enjoy it fresh, when the cloves are mature but not dried. Green garlic is also used, cut up like scallion tops.

In any case, garlic lovers are quite likely to use a shocking amount of the stuff.

In addition to fresh onions and garlic, chili ingredients often contain onion or garlic salt, powder, flakes (dried), juice, and so on. I've even seen canned onion soup listed as an ingredient. All of these are acceptable, but fresh onions and garlic are usually better.

For cooking purposes I am fond of wild onions and wild garlic, including ramps, a sort of leek that grows wild in the Appalachians.

Usually these have a small but strongly flavored bulb—too strong for eating raw as a topping—but they are great for cooking if used in moderation. The stalk can also be chopped and used like chives. One variety or another of wild onions and garlic grows all over the country in great plenty, even in yards and along roadways. Note also that some of these plants form a cluster of little bulblets atop the flowering knee-high stems. These can be picked by the handful and used without further preparation in chili. What could be easier?

THE VEGETABLE GARDEN

A die-hard champion of Texas chili once said that the Californians tend to throw in the whole vegetable garden. It's true, although I suspect that the California boys, at least those considerably south of San Francisco, add a lot of outlandish stuff just to rile the Texans again. In any case, I've found chili recipes containing everything from artichokes to zucchini. Even spinach. And pumpkin. One recipe called for red cabbage—another for 2 cups of sauerkraut! Chopped carrots, eggplant, green beans, and so on. Cactus pads. Even olives and capers, along with such vegetable flavorings as horseradish and gingerroot. While most of this stuff will cook away and disappear during long, slow simmering, and will surely be overpowered by the flavor of cumin and the heat of capsaicin, fast cooking may leave it intact, recognizable, and laughable to almost everybody except vegans and vegetarians and uptight white-hat chefs.

Apart from peppers, tomatoes, and onions (all covered earlier), the only other vegetable taken seriously as a chili ingredient is celery, and this by only a few jackleg cooks. It's not a regional thing—I have seen recipes from Florida to Alaska that called for it. See the Chili According to Ed Martley recipe in chapter 14, in which the celery helps in the cooking process and is quite obviously considered indispensable. A friend of mine, a game warden, watched me carefully when he revealed that celery was an important ingredient in his chili. I wasn't too surprised. In any case, celery seeds are also used in chili recipes, as are chopped celery leaves.

Potatoes are not normally used in chili, but they can be useful for soaking up salt and spices used in excess. Small new potatoes, of course, can be cooked in thin chili, or perhaps served on the side.

Mushrooms? Naw. Not with chili, although a few recipes call for them. If you are a culinary sport with money to spare, however, or perhaps an adventurous farmer, you might add quite a bit of cuitlacoche, which is quite expensive these days in gourmet markets. See my Gourmet Cuitlacoche Chili recipe in chapter 15.

FRUITS AND JUICES

I feel that fruits are better served as a chili go-with (except for the tomato, which is technically a fruit), but don't be surprised to see them listed in some recipes. I have seen several ingredients lists called for dried fruits—even prunes and raisins—as well as various fruit condiments, such as cranberry sauce. One recipe calls for a full cup of applesauce.

Lemon and lime juice are sometimes called for in chili recipes, often used during the serving phase. Some sports add slices of lemon or lime into the pot. And—you guessed it—lemon, lime, and orange zest are getting into the act these days.

SPICES AND HERBS

I get the feeling that many chili cooks simply look through the spice rack and add a little of this or that on whim, or at least without much thought. Others insist that basil or some such herb really makes a superior chili. While very small amounts of this stuff won't hurt much and won't overpower the all-important flavor of cumin, it is usually a waste of time and money. All spices are expensive unless you grow your own. Personally, I'm far too frugal to buy something like mace just to put ½ teaspoon into a big pot of chili, knowing that the rest of the bottle or tin will most likely sit in the spice rack until it loses its flavor and should be discarded.

In the what-ya-got category, I have seen recipes calling for small measures of everything from rosemary to sweet woodruff. It's not unusual to see a chili recipe calling for 30 ingredients these days, many of which are spices. Who will know if you leave out ⅛ teaspoon of ground coriander? Who would know if you add a pinch of germander?

If you are going to use spices and herbs effectively, they should be fresh. Even the dried herbs tend to lose their strength after long storage. The general rule is that they should be replaced after six months. I have kept them for a year after opening the jar—and in other kitchens I've seen them sit for six or seven years. And who knows how long they sat on the supermarket shelf?

In any case, it's best to store spices in a tightly sealed jar or container in a cool, dry place. The refrigerator is good, if you've got room and can devise an easy way to find them. It's also best, in almost all cases, to store seeds and spice corns in the whole form, then grind them as needed. Freshly ground spices have more flavor and aroma. This includes black pepper berries, allspice, and even salt. A mortar and pestle is hard to beat for grinding.

In any case, here are a few spices and herbs that figure into the chili recipe for one reason or another.

Cumin. As I hope I have made clear, cumin is the dominant spice in modern chili, especially if you consider the chile pepper as a vegetable. Even if you use hot chile powder as a spice, its flavor is usually, in most recipes, overpowered by cumin. This Old World spice is available as seeds or as a powder. Seeds store better, tending to hold the flavor until cooked or ground. Store either cumin seeds or powder in a cool, dry, dark place.

Oregano. A member of the mint family, oregano is frequently used in chili recipes. It is not as important as cumin, but it has become almost traditional. But not quite. Some of us, including myself, don't always use it, especially in recipes that contain no tomato. In any case, oregano is kin to both thyme and marjoram. In fact, it is sometimes called wild marjoram. Two kinds are available.

European or Mediterranean oregano, which has a stronger flavor than marjoram and isn't as sweet, is marketed in regular supermarket spice selections, either in dried form or as a powder. Fresh oregano is also available here and there. As a rule, any supermarket oregano will be of the European kind, unless otherwise specified on the package.

The second kind, Mexican oregano, available in Latin markets and in larger spice selections, is stronger than European and is often preferred by some chiliheads. Use it sparingly. Mexican oregano is a different species from regular oregano. It is also called Mexican marjoram or wild Mexican sage.

Note that oregano goes nicely with tomato-based dishes. Keep this in mind when adding lots of tomatoes to your chili recipe. Also remember that oregano has a limited shelf life, especially after the container has been opened. Store it in a cool, dark place.

Salt. I consider salt essential in chili, and I like to add it at the beginning of the simmering phase simply because I enjoy tasting as I stir. Adding it to individual bowls as wanted will do if you are feeding people who have a problem with salt, or who fear it. Ordinary table salt is fine for chili, but I prefer a large sea salt that can be ground to size in a small mill. This salt, now available in a dozen kinds, some of which are quite expensive, contains more minerals of the sea and more flavor than "refined" table salt.

Black Pepper. Black pepper adds an excellent flavor to chili, especially if it is freshly ground. Owing to its aroma as it comes from the pepper mill, I like to grind a few twists directly into the bowl, atop the red before other toppings are added.

Red Pepper. This ground hot pepper, usually called cayenne, adds a kick to a bowl of red and is often used as a spice along with other ground chile powder or chili powder. It is made from cayenne pepper or any of several hot red peppers originally grown in the Cayenne area of French Guiana.

Epazote. This herb grows wild in some areas. In the past, dried epazote has been available mainly in Latin markets, but it is becoming more widely stocked by spice merchants everywhere. Traditionally, it is popular in bean dishes because it is believed to reduce gas. This fits right in with chili, which often contains not only beans but also onions. Personally, I don't need epazote and I have never taken to its pungent, strong flavor.

Annatto (Achiote) Seeds and Powder. This red-orange stuff is used mainly as a coloring agent, but it does have a subtle flavor. I think the flavor is completely subdued by cumin, and the color really isn't needed in a bowl of red if enough chile pulp has been used. It is, however, not an uncommon ingredient in chili recipes. As usual, the seeds store better than the ground form. In general, annatto is more important in commercial applications (as a coloring agent) and in the cookery of the Yucatán.

Allspice. This great spice from the West Indies and South America combines the flavors of cinnamon, nutmeg, and cloves. Hence, the name "allspice." I always look very closely at any recipe that calls for allspice *and* cinnamon, nutmeg, and clove. In any case, it's a small berry from the pimiento tree. It's also called Jamaican pepper and is an important ingredient in island jerk spice mixes. Although it is frequently used as an ingredient in chili—especially in Midwest- and Cincinnati-style recipes—it really doesn't add much to a bowl of red if used in small amounts, but it won't hurt much, either. Allspice stores much better as whole berries, then ground as needed.

Parsley and Cilantro. These herbs are often used, especially in the fresh form, as a garnish or sprinkling to top a bowl of red, and some people consider them ingredients to be added during the cooking phase. In parts of Southeast Asia, cilantro is almost a vegetable instead of a mere herb, and the roots are used as well as the leaves. For some reason, cilantro, the Old World plant whose berries are called coriander, has become almost a required addition to highly spiced dishes. In chili use it sparingly, if at all.

Bay Leaves. Because I like the aroma of bay leaves in a simmering stew, I often put two or three leaves into a bowl of chili that is to be cooked for a long time, holding back on the cumin and other spices until near the end of the cooking period. Before serving, the bay leaves should be fished out and discarded. Yeah, yeah, I know. I'm guilty of adding to the list of chili ingredients. But at least bay leaves are easy to measure, and I use them for a very good purpose—for the cook to enjoy.

Spice Mixes. These days spice mixes take up as much space in supermarkets as pure spices. We've got all manner of rubs and seasoned salts, such as lemon-pepper and fajita seasoning and taco mixes and Cajun dust, along with such foreign mixes as the French *quatre epices* and the Mongolian *biriyani masala*. Even Worcestershire *powder*. Most of this stuff becomes mere clutter for the spice rack, not serious additions to a bowl of red.

Of course, the chili mixes (chapter 4) can be quite useful and economical (as compared to buying half a dozen spices for making your own mix), and a good mix will help cook up an excellent bowl of chili with only four or five ingredients to measure.

Monosodium Glutamate. This stuff, often called MSG, became something of a culinary fad a few decades ago. Although it has lost favor in recent years, it is still sold in the spice sections of supermarkets, often under names like Ac'cent, and it is present in many seasoning mixes. MSG doesn't impart its own flavor to food; rather, it seems to intensity the flavors already present. It is commonly seen in chili recipes, but I seldom use it myself. Good chili made with plenty of chile powder and a little cumin doesn't need boosting.

Filé. This spice, used to flavor and thicken soups and stews, is sometimes specified in chili recipes. I want to point out that this stuff—powdered sassafras leaves—will somehow turn a stew into a stringy mess if cooked at high temperature. I do not recommend putting it in a pot of chili that is still on the heat or that will be reheated. It's best to sprinkle a little into each bowl, if it is used at all.

SAUCES AND CONDIMENTS

A good many jackleg cooks put Worcestershire sauce in just about everything. A few others add, in addition to the Worcestershire and catsup, prepared horseradish, mustard, and so on. These days the most popular condiment, outselling even catsup, is tomato-based salsa. These sauces, usually available in hot, medium, or mild, can be an excellent addition to chili, but it's the sort of thing we add without it being in the ingredients list. Many other tomato-based sauces are also used, as discussed under the tomato heading above.

Perhaps the most popular condiment for chili is a hot pepper sauce, such as Tabasco, made from red Tabasco peppers, or Louisiana hot sauce, usually made from red cayenne peppers. There must be a thousand of these sauces in the world, usually with some outrageous name such as Scorned Woman, and all have one thing in common: a hefty shot of capsaicin. Although these can be added during the cooking phase, they work best as a finishing sauce to add heat as needed, or as a table shake-bottle sauce.

One British chili recipe calls for ½ cup of chutney, an East Indian condiment usually made with fruit, vinegar, sugar, and spices. It is quite popular with curry dishes—and curry, like chili, relies heavily on cumin. Hence, its use as a chili go-with isn't too far-fetched, I guess.

Other condiments sometimes used in chili include olives and capers. Even peanuts. In West Texas, mesquite blossoms are sometimes used as an ingredient.

Sweets, Bitters, and Sours

A surprising range of flavorings are used in chili recipes, including Angostura bitters, vinegar, lemon juice, and various sweets. Ideally, these should be added to help achieve a desired effect or to make up for something that is missing in the recipe, based on the cook's knowledge and taste, not on his whim or imagination. Otherwise, the ingredients lists of our recipes will continue to get longer and longer and longer.

Sweets. These are said to balance the heat of the chile peppers and bring out the other flavors. Some add white sugar; others, brown. Me, I like the taste of truly unrefined sugar, such as the Mexican piloncillo cones. (Supermarket brown sugar is merely refined white sugar with molasses added.) Blackstrap molasses and various syrups are also called for in some recipes. Even maple syrup. I like a pure sugarcane syrup, for the same reason that I prefer unrefined brown sugar. Sweet chocolate is also used in a surprising number of recipes, but unsweetened bitter chocolate is probably more popular, as discussed in the next heading.

In any case, one food writer has recommended a minimum of 1 tablespoon of sugar for a pot of chili designed to feed six people. He goes on, saying that with too much sugar you have dessert; too little, you have turpentine. I disagree, having never detected a hint of turpentine in a bowl of my chili, always made without sweeteners except when I am testing recipes. I might add that anyone who uses lots of onions in his chili should know that they contain quite a bit of sugar.

Honey is often used in recipes, and, of course, regional favorites are called for, such as mesquite honey in Texas and tupelo honey in my part of Florida (Wewahitchka, home of the annual Tupelo Festival). There is some difference, I allow, between one honey and another—but when it goes up against cumin, one honey is pretty much the same as another. Just don't overdo it. I have read that the California Honey Advisory Board published a chili recipe that called for ¼ cup of honey to 1½ pounds of meat. That's too sweet for me.

Bitters. Bitter chocolate or unsweetened cocoa powder adds a certain texture as well as the bitter principle to chili. This may sound strange to some people, but the similar uses of chocolate date back to the Aztecs, who used it in such dishes as the famous *guajolote con mole poblano.* The upper-crust Aztecs prohibited the womenfolk to partake of chocolate, but remember that times have changed and these days many women tend to stuff themselves with the stuff as if to satisfy a long craving. In any case, both chocolate and cocoa are not uncommon in modern chili recipes. In some recipes, I'll swear, cocoa powder is used as a garnish, sprinkled over the sour cream.

See also the bitters recipe in chapter 15.

Sours. I understand that Craig Claiborne, once food editor for the *New York Times,* wrote a thinking man's chili recipe that called for vinegar and two slices of fresh lime to be added during the cooking phase. Both the vinegar and lime tend to negate the need for salt in low-sodium recipes, which were popular a few years back. A number of people also serve vinegar on the side in cruets, to be used to taste, and lemon (or lime) wedges are also served as garnish. Both tend to cut the grease off the spoon.

Believe-It-or-Nots. Fire ants have a bitter acidic taste, and I have seen chili recipes calling for them. I understand that some town in Texas once required a few fire ants in any recipe used in its chili cook-off. In any case, an ant or two makes for good conversation and won't hurt a thing in chili that is long simmered. Even better than fire ants would be the honey ants that live in the Southwest. These ants feed on honey exuded from oak galls and store it, not in a comb, but inside repletes. These are large ants that hang upside down in the hill and store the honey in their huge abdomens, which swell to grotesque size. The Indians of old relished these replete honey ants.

In any case, remember that you don't really have to put fire ants into the chili. If you don't have one or two at hand, lie about it. That's what the Texans do.

7

GREEN CHILI

Long popular in the Southwest, green chili stew has become more and more acceptable around the country and now enjoys a somewhat minor category in chili cook-offs in some parts. I think the stew owes its popularity in part to the current craze for roasted green peppers and the general atavistic yearning for burned stuff, including grilled meats, caramelized onions and other skillet fare, and "fire-roasted" vegetables. These days we even see recipes for Fire-Roasted Mayonnaise. In any case, green chili stew is very good stuff, but I doubt it will ever reach the popularity of the red. For one thing, it's very different—and it doesn't always contain cumin.

It's best to use fresh peppers for green chili, but canned will do if you can find them in economical sizes. Most of the supermarket brands will be marketed in small cans—usually 8 ounces or less—and can often be found in the Mexican food section. The persistent cook, however, can find green chiles in 16-ounce cans or jars, or even larger. While working on this text, for example, I found some green chiles from Hatch, New Mexico (home of the annual Chile Festival), packaged in 27-ounce cans, and available by mail order.

Roasted Green Chili

Fresh pork shoulder works well in green chili recipes, although other meats can also be used. Avoid cured ham, however. The ingredients list for this recipe calls for a large Boston butt, but the picnic ham can also be used. In either case, bone the meat, remove most of the fat, and chop the meat into 1-inch chunks. A large Boston butt of 5 or 6 pounds will yield about 3 pounds of chopped meat. Half a pound more or less won't hurt the recipe.

    3 pounds fresh pork chunks
    10–12 poblano chile peppers
    1 or more green cayenne or jalapeño peppers
    1 large onion, chopped
    5 cloves garlic, minced
    2 cups chicken stock
    ¼ cup cooking oil (more if needed)
    salt and freshly ground black pepper to taste
    1 teaspoon freshly ground cumin
    ½ teaspoon dried oregano
    freshly ground white cornmeal (optional)

Roast, seed, and chop the poblano peppers. Chop the cayenne or jalapeño, seeds and all. Set the peppers aside but keep separate. Heat about half the oil in a cast-iron stovetop Dutch oven. Sauté the chopped onion and garlic for 5 minutes. Remove with a slotted spoon and set aside. Brown the meat lightly, working in two or more batches. Use more oil if needed, depending in part on how fatty the meat is. Put all the meat into the pot, along with the sautéed onion and garlic. Stir in the chopped poblano peppers, half the cayenne peppers with seeds, the chicken stock, salt, pepper, cumin, and oregano. Bring to a light boil, reduce the heat to very low, cover, and simmer for several hours. Stir from time to time, taste for seasonings, and add a little more of the chopped cayenne if needed for hotness. Add a little water or more chicken stock if needed; or thicken with a little cornmeal. Serve hot with rolled cornmeal tortillas, cowboy beans, and vine-ripened tomatoes on the side. Boiled new potatoes also go nicely with this dish.

Zuñi Green Chili

Chile peppers and hominy (whole-kernel corn without skins, as the Native Americans call it) are important in the cookery of the southwestern Native Americans. Hominy can be made at home, but it's much easier these days to buy it in cans, available in white or yellow, or dried, available in white, yellow, and purple. Ordinary bell peppers from the supermarket or home garden will work for this recipe, but I prefer to use a large Mexican chile such as poblano (these, when dried, are called ancho), which are quite mild. For heat, I use a couple of jalapeños. In a pinch, use a teaspoon of ordinary red pepper flakes, available in any supermarket. A crushed red pepper such as cayenne can be used, or try a wild bird pepper if you have one. This recipe has been adapted rather freely from The Art of American Indian Cooking, *which listed boned lamb for the meat. It will do. So will goat shoulder. The Native Americans, however, used pronghorn or deer before the Spanish brought them sheep and cows (and horses). The juniper berry was an important seasoning for the Native Americans, and they are now available in the spice markets and some upscale supermarkets. You can also pick and dry your own. The Native Americans, I understand, cook this stew as a ceremonial dish, and the Pueblos are said to keep a pot bubbling in case anyone drops in to visit. Talk about potluck!*

    3 pounds pronghorn shoulder meat
    1 (16-ounce) can white hominy
    1 (16-ounce) can yellow hominy
    6 mild green chile peppers, medium to large
    2 medium hot green peppers (jalapeño)
    2 medium onions, chopped

2 cloves garlic, crushed
6 dried juniper berries, crushed
½ cup minced fresh parsley or cilantro
2 teaspoons dried Mexican oregano
cooking oil
flour
hot water
salt and freshly ground black pepper to taste

Seed, stem, and chop all the green peppers. Cut the meat into 1½-inch cubes, trimming any sinew or fat as you go. Shake the meat in a brown bag with some flour. Heat a little oil in a skillet, using just enough to cover the bottom by about ¹⁄₁₆ inch. Brown the meat a little at a time in several batches, adding a little more oil if needed. Put the browned meat into a stovetop Dutch oven. Add more oil to the skillet and sauté the onions until they start to brown around the edges. Stir in the chopped green peppers, garlic, crushed juniper berries, parsley, oregano, black pepper, and salt. Add to the browned meat in the Dutch oven. Pour in enough hot water to cover. Bring to a boil, cover tightly, reduce the heat to very low, and simmer for at least 1½ hours (longer if practical), or until the meat is very tender. Add more water as needed and stir from time to time to keep the bottom from sticking. During the last hour of cooking, stir in the canned hominy, drained. Stir and cook and taste, adding more salt and black pepper if needed. Serve hot in bowls, along with plenty of soft corn tortillas on the side, rolled for easy sopping. Use leftover chili for stuffing squash blossoms.

Variation: During the last hour of cooking, stir in two chopped green tomatoes.

Easy Skillet Chili Verdes

Here's a quick no-fuss dish, made with canned chiles. I list ground chuck of beef, but any good meat can be used.

    1 pound ground chuck
    1 (8-ounce) can tomato sauce
    1 (8-ounce) can green chili sauce
    1 (4-ounce) can diced green chiles
    1 large onion, diced
    2 cloves garlic, diced
    ½ teaspoon freshly ground black pepper
    ¼ teaspoon oregano
    bacon drippings or cooking oil
    salt to taste
    water or beef stock, if needed

Heat a little of the bacon drippings or oil in a large skillet, barely covering the bottom. Brown the onion and garlic; strain and set aside. Brown the ground meat and pour off the fat. Add the sautéed onion and garlic back to the skillet, along with the rest of the ingredients. Stir with a wooden spoon. Reduce the heat to very low and simmer for about 30 minutes, stirring from time to time. Add a little water or stock as needed. Serve hot in bowls. Feeds 2 to 4.

Taos Old-Time Roast Pork Green Chili

This old recipe from New Mexico starts off with cooking a whole pork roast, then using it in a green chili. A friend named Daryl passed the recipe on to me, saying she got it from a Norteño named Mopé, part Pueblo and part

New Mexican, who worked at a restaurant in Taos. It calls for lots of canned or fresh whole green chiles, which Daryl specified as Number 6, peeled. I tested it out with 10 pounds of fresh poblano chiles (which I happened to have in my garden), roasted, seeded, and peeled. Good stuff.

THE ROAST

1 pork roast (5–6 pounds)
10 large cans whole green chiles (see alternative above)
5–6 medium onions, chopped
5–6 tablespoons minced garlic
3 tablespoons ground cumin
salt and black pepper to taste
cayenne to taste, if needed

Put the pork roast and all the ingredients into a roasting bag (spread out in a roasting pan) and bake in a 300° oven for several hours, or until the pork falls apart. Discard the roasting bag and chop the roast meat, mixing it into the contents of the roasting pan as you go. Keep warm.

THE CHILI

4–5 pounds ground beef or venison
1 large onion, chopped
3 tablespoons cooking oil
4–5 tablespoons flour
hot water

In a large Dutch oven or other suitable pot, heat the oil and brown the onion. Stir in the flour a little at a time. Add the ground meat and stir until lightly browned. Add the chopped pork and the contents of the baking pan, along with enough water to barely cover. Simmer for an hour, stirring and tasting from time to time. Add a little more water if needed. Serve hot. Enjoy—and dig in for seconds.

Garlic Chili

Here's a recipe adapted from The Garlic Lover's Cookbook, *calling for three heads. Not cloves. Whole heads—up to thirty cloves. It calls for green chiles, and I assume that Anaheims or New Mexicos will do. The green tomatoes are a happy addition, at least to me. No cumin is used, which is all right for a green chili, I think. Another surprise is that the beef can be cut into* slices *or into the more traditional cubes.*

    2 pounds beef
    3 heads fresh garlic
    6 fresh green chiles, diced
    3 large green tomatoes, diced
    1 large onion, diced
    ½ cup olive oil
    ½ teaspoon salt
    ½ teaspoon white pepper

Separate the garlic heads into cloves, peel, and set aside. Cut the beef into ½-inch cubes or slices, like stir-fry meat. Heat the oil in a large skillet and cook the meat until it is tender. Place the whole garlic cloves into the skillet with the meat and cook until tender. Add the diced chiles, onion, and tomatoes, along with the salt and pepper. Cover and simmer until the chiles and onion are tender. Serve hot.

PART TWO

Meats for Chili

As a rule, the inexpensive cuts of meat are the best for chili, partly because they are tougher and stand up better to long, slow simmering. Indeed, turning a sorry cut of meat into something as good as chili gives the cook an added sense of accomplishment unobtainable with tenderloin.

Although most modern recipes for chili call for regular ground meat, many chiliheads insist that a special coarse grind is much better. This is called a chili grind. Many kitchen sausage grinders can be fitted with cutting plates to produce several sizes of grind, from fine up to ½ inch or larger. Grinding meat with these machines really isn't difficult, and gives the chili cook the added satisfaction of knowing what exactly is in the meat. Some recipes call for half ground meat and half diced meat, both in beef or sometimes ground beef and diced pork, or whatever.

Many chili cooks prefer to cut the meat into small cubes (usually ¼ to ½ inch) with a knife. I count myself among these. Large chunks of meat can be reduced, or you can purchase stew meat at the market and reduce each piece as required.

Also remember that partly frozen meat is easier to slice—and don't forget to sharpen the knife. A sharp paring knife will work better than a dull butcher's knife.

Although beef is very popular for chili, any good red or even white meat can be used. Venison is my choice, either from the hunt or from one of the many commercial game farms that are becoming more popular around the country. A tough old buck, difficult to cook by quick methods and dry-heat grilling, will do just fine for chili. So will some of the modern exotic meats, such as buffalo and ostrich.

Meats suitable for chili are covered further in chapters that follow.

8

CHILI WITH BEEF

Ground beef is not a bad choice for chili, partly because it's readily available and relatively inexpensive. It's easy to prepare for the pot and can be cooked quickly, if need be.

I'm not offering recipes in this chapter, except for an old cowboy delicacy at the end, because most of the recipes in other sections of this book call for beef. Instead, here are a few topics to consider, bearing in mind that the prime beef for steaks and grilling is not the best choice for chili. A tough cut of beef is better than loin or tenderloin *if* you have the time and patience to cook it on low heat for a long time—and a tough range cow is better than a tender feedlot specimen for chili. Some chiliheads insist on having the old Texas longhorns (still available in a few markets) instead of a modern breed like Black Angus. Other sports insist on other kinds of beef, and a British recipe calls for Scotch beef. I've never seen the Japanese Kobe beef (massaged with sake and fed beer) specified in a recipe, but I wouldn't be too surprised to see it in a chili book.

Anyhow, here's my breakdown:

Market Hamburger. Often made from scraps from various cuts of meat, market hamburger usually contains quite a bit of fat. It is inexpensive and makes a good chili, and is especially useful for greasy-spoon recipes. While most people will want to cut back on the fat these days, a few chiliheads insist that lots of fat is essential for good chili. And no one can deny that it is quite filling and very nutritious, quite suited as a high-energy cold-weather food. What it does to one's cholesterol count is another matter.

Ground Chuck. This is ground meat from the forequarter of the cow. It is made from various trimmings and from the shanks. Being relatively high in fat and flavor, it makes a purely excellent chili—probably the best of the market grinds.

Ground Round. This is ground meat from the hindquarter, including the shin. It is relatively low in fat, but it makes an excellent chili.

Chili Grind. Coarsely ground beef (or other meat) marketed mostly for chili. It may be available in a few meat markets, or perhaps on special order. The best bet is to grind your own, remembering that many kitchen sausage mills have optional plates for grinding fine or coarse meat, ranging from ⅛ inch up to ½ inch. The larger-sized plate is used for chili grind.

Steaks. Most steaks suitable for grilling are not ideal for chili. Round steak will do, and chuck steak is better, if you want a little more fat. Yeah, I know that many chile recipes call for loin steaks of one sort or another, and the author of a modern chili book seems to favor leftover grilled rib eyes! (Who has leftover grilled rib eyes?) I've seen three kinds of tender steaks called for in the same recipe. All of these good meats can, of course, be used to make good chili—but they tend to take away some of the cook's satisfaction of making a good bowl of red from sorry meats. Generally, such tender cuts do not require long cooking (which, indeed, tends to cook the meat apart) and can therefore be good choices if you are in a hurry.

Chuck. This cut of beef, from the shoulder, is full of flavor and contains quite a bit of fat marbled in the grain. It makes an excellent chili. Cut it into ½-inch cubes or larger. Fine cubes may tend to cook away.

Brisket. This tough, fatty slab of meat, weighing about 20 pounds on a mature cow, is often used for making corned beef or barbecue. It can be ground and diced for chili, if you need a large batch. If the brisket isn't on display in your meat market, talk to the butcher. Don't let him sell you a slab of corned beef, which, although made from the brisket, is very different from fresh meat. Also keep in mind that the brisket can be divided into two parts: the point cut, which contains quite a bit of fat, and the flat cut, which is leaner and less flavorful.

Hind Leg. A leg of beef contains several cuts of meat and muscles. Usually these are cut into steaks (such as round steak) or chops and roasts of one sort of another. These cuts are usually sold in small packages, but often sirloin tips (a somewhat triangular roast from the hip or rump, the section between the leg and the loin) and such cuts can be purchased. Unless you want a large chunk of meat, the best bet is to buy round steak (usually cut about ½ inch thick) or one of the thinner convenience cuts, as discussed below.

Convenience Cuts. There are several cuts of beef that make for easy dicing. Stew meat, although usually cut into fairly large chunks, can be reduced quickly with a sharp paring knife. Stir-fry strips are even easier and need only be bunched together and sliced crosswise. Several of the small cutlets such as breakfast steaks are usually quite thin and can be cut first into strips and then into cubes; with a sharp knife, simply make cuts lengthwise and cross-wise, checkerboard style.

Shanks and Shins. These are the smaller parts of the front and hind legs, and are perhaps the best of the cow for making chili. Unfortunately, many of our modern meat markets and supermarkets never receive these cuts. They are removed at the meatpacking house, where they are ground into burger. Usually the shank, from the front leg, is used for ground chuck; the shin, from the rear, for ground round. If you can find a butcher who can provide a shank, which will weigh between 10 and 20 pounds, try it, cooked for long time in water and a little chopped celery. When the meat is very tender, bone it and put it back into the pot. Strain the stock. Cut the bone into several pieces so that the marrow can easily cook out and contribute to the stock. (Remember that the term "osso bucco," made from veal shank, means "cracked bone.") If you must deal with the bone at home without a meat saw, try a hacksaw for cutting or a heavy hammer for cracking.

Beef Heart. This is one of the toughest muscles in the cow. When trimmed and reduced to ½-inch dice, it makes a very good chili with a slightly chewy texture, even after long simmering. In some meat markets, the hearts can be purchased fresh or frozen at reasonable prices, but they are not normal supermarket fare.

Other Bovine Organs. Beef tongue can be used to make a good chili, but it's really better when merely boiled, sliced, and served with a good brown mustard. Forget the cow liver and most other innards for chili, except for the heart, covered above, and an old delicacy called mountain oysters. Here's the recipe.

Cowboy Chili

This is a cowboy recipe to cook at calf branding and cutting time, in a pot over the coals used to heat the irons. According to Bill Bridges, Will Rogers' favorite chili was made with calf fries. Others might argue for lamb fries or pig fries, or maybe those from white-tailed deer or bull moose. Those who don't eat fries of any sort might want to try the recipe with beef heart.

    2 pounds calf fries
    1 large onion, chopped
    4 cloves garlic, minced

¼ cup pure ancho chile powder
1–2 tablespoons cumin seeds
½ tablespoon red pepper flakes
2 tablespoons rendered suet or lard
salt and black pepper to taste
flour
water

Wash, skin, and dice the fries. Heat the rendered suet or lard in a deep skillet with a tight lid. Lightly brown the fries, a few at a time. Add the onions, garlic, cumin seeds, and red pepper flakes. Cook uncovered for 4 or 5 minutes, until the onions are soft. Stir in the ancho powder, salt, and black pepper. Barely cover with water, bring to a boil, cover tightly, and simmer for at least 2 hours, stirring and adding more water as needed from time to time. A few minutes before you are ready to eat, mix a little flour and water, making a paste. Stir in some of this, a little at a time, until the chili is as thick as you like it. Taste and adjust salt and pepper, if necessary. Yee-haw!

9

CHILI WITH PORK

Although fresh pork is sometimes used in chili, it works best as a second meat to beef or some other red meat. There are exceptions, especially in the green chili recipes in chapter 7. Often cured pork is used as a sort of seasoning, and some recipes call for bacon, hog jowls, and ham hocks. Sausage is a fairly common ingredient in chili, and a few recipes call for sausage as the only meat. (Most of the sausages are made from pork, but a few, such as kosher salami, call for other meats.)

Jarrod's Three-Cheer Chili with Hoop Cheese

Here's a recipe for a mild chili as cooked and served in a beach house on St. George's Island. Made to feed a family with diverse tastes, it wasn't too spicy and didn't reek of cumin. Good stuff. For the topping, use only red-rind hoop cheese, Jarrod says. It's always best, I say, to use unrefrigerated red-rind hoop cheese, if you can find it these days. In general, hoop cheese is simply a Wisconsin cheddar. It was once available in country stores, unrefrigerated, of course. Wedges were cut out from the hoop as needed. These days hoop cheese is available mostly in supermarkets, almost always precut and packaged in small wedges—and, sadly, almost always refrigerated.

    1 pound ground beef
    1 pound bulk pork sausage

1 pound smoked pork sausage, sliced
2 (16-ounce) cans tomatoes, diced
2 (16-ounce) cans dark red kidney beans
1 cup fresh mushrooms, diced
1 medium red onion, diced
6 cloves garlic, diced
1 packet chili seasoning
3 tablespoons chili powder
3 tablespoons dried oregano
½ tablespoon Tabasco Sauce
water as needed
coarsely grated hoop cheese

In a large cast-iron skillet, brown the ground beef, bulk sausage, and pork sausage, stirring as you go with a wooden spoon. Add the onion, garlic, and mushrooms. Cook and stir until the onion is transparent. Add the tomatoes, kidney beans, and water. Bring to a light boil, stirring in the rest of the ingredients, all except for the Tabasco Sauce and cheese. Reduce the heat to medium low and simmer for 30 minutes, stirring and tasting from time to time. Add Tabasco if you want it hotter, or put a shake bottle on the table for individual use. (I'll take a little freshly ground black pepper on mine.) Serve hot with saltine crackers, topping each bowl with grated hoop cheese. It is permissible to crumble a short stack of crackers into each bowl. Three cheers for Jarrod.

Ham Hock Chili with Beans from Scratch

Nothing seasons a pot of beans better than smoked ham hocks. Available in most grocery stores these days, usually cut into lengths of about 2½ inches, these contain lots of bone, fat, and connective tissue, all of which make for

a rich stock. I like to cook this recipe with dried pinto beans along with the
ham hocks and venison or tough beef.

2 pounds diced venison or tough beef
2 pounds ham hocks
1 pound pinto beans
1 large onion, chopped
4 cloves garlic, crushed
4–6 tablespoons chili powder
red pepper flakes to taste
salt and black pepper to taste
water as needed

Put the ham hocks into a suitable pot, cover well with water, bring to a boil, reduce the heat to simmer, and cook for a couple of hours, or until the meat is falling off. Bone the meat and put it back into the pot, discarding the bones, skin, and gristle. Add the pinto beans, diced venison, onion, garlic, chili powder, red pepper flakes, salt, and pepper. Cover well with water, remembering that the pinto beans will absorb moisture and expand as they cook. Bring to a new boil, reduce the heat, cover tightly, and simmer for 3 hours or so, stirring and adding more water from time to time as needed. Serve this one with corn pone, sliced Vidalia onions, and thick slices of vine-ripened tomatoes.

Bacon-Seasoned Chili

This is more a technique than a recipe, because it can be used in most chili recipes that call for cooking oil or bacon drippings to help brown the meat.

2 pounds venison or lean beef
¼ pound smoked bacon
1 medium-to-large onion, diced
1 large tomato, diced
3 tablespoons chili powder
salt and black pepper to taste
water
sour cream (for topping)

Fry the bacon in a skillet until crisp. Drain the bacon, crumble it, and set it aside. In the drippings, brown the venison or beef and onion. Add the tomato and enough water to cover the meat. Stir in the chili powder, salt, and black pepper. Bring to a boil, reduce the heat to very low, cover, and simmer for 2 hours or longer, depending on how tough the meat is and on how much time you have. The longer the better, within reason. Stir and add more water from time to time, if needed. Serve hot in bowls. Top each serving with a dollop of sour cream and sprinkle with the reserved bacon bits.

10

CHILI WITH VENISON

Now we're cooking. If the animal has been properly field-dressed and duly cooled, venison is the perfect meat for chili that is to be simmered for a long time. If the meat has not been properly handled, however, not even cumin will get rid of the gamy taste. Sometimes a large buck in rut will have an off taste, and chasing the deer all over the country with dogs or otherwise riling it before the kill will give the meat a strong flavor. But usually the meat has no bad taste or odor.

Most venison is on the tough side, being lean and dry. So, why not cut out the loin and tenderloin for chops, then grind or dice the rest of the meat for chili and sausage making? Some of the large pots used for boiling crab or frying a whole turkey can be used to cook large batches of chili, or the meat can be frozen in 2- or 5-pound packages (preferably in vacuum-pack plastic bags) for use in standard recipes.

The whitetail is by far America's most popular big-game animal, and in some areas they are considered pests. Of course, the mule deer and others, including the large elk and moose, also make good chili. So will caribou.

Easy Deer Camp Chili

*Making a pot of chili in camp is made easy with the commercial chili powders
and chili mixes, some of which are available in any supermarket, but I still think
it's better to start with pure ground chile and cumin. The mix can be made at
home, so that measurements in camp aren't necessary. Because venison is very
lean, a little fat helps the chili. So, if you don't have some fatty sausage, add some
bacon drippings or even cooking oil to brown the meat.*

2 pounds venison or other game
½ pound venison sausage with some pork fat
1 medium-to-large onion, chopped
⅓ cup ancho or New Mexico chile powder
2 teaspoons ground cumin seeds, or to taste
salt and black pepper to taste
springwater

Cut the sausage into ½-inch wheels and the venison into ½-inch
dice. Brown the sausage in a pot, trying out a little of the fat. Brown
the venison and onion. Sprinkle on the spices, stirring as you go.
Add enough water to cover. Bring to a boil. Reduce the heat to
very low, cover tightly, and simmer for 3 or 4 hours, or longer if
you've got the time. Be sure to stir and add a little water from time
to time as needed. Serve hot with crackers. Rice or beans can be
served on the side, or mixed into the chili. If using canned beans,
stir them into the chill during the last 10 minutes of cooking.

Dr. Hodges' Buzzard Breath Chili

*By chilihead standards, this good stew isn't nearly as potent as it sounds.
I've seen several versions of the "buzzard breath" recipe, and this one has*

been adapted from a Ducks Unlimited cookbook. The recipe contains some inexact measures such as "2 cans tomato sauce" without specifying the size of the can. Also, I have changed "2 cans mushrooms" to 8 ounces fresh mushrooms, which are widely available these days in supermarkets. The mushrooms can also be omitted, noting that they are not standard ingredients for chili. Note that the recipe doesn't contain much chili powder, which, in turn, means that it doesn't contain much cumin. Taste it toward the end of the cooking. If it doesn't taste the way you think chili ought to, add some cumin powder.

    2 cups deerburger (venison ground with some pork fat)
    2 cups chopped onions
    1½ cups chopped green pepper
    2 (16-ounce) cans kidney beans
    2 (16-ounce) cans tomatoes
    2 (8-ounce) cans tomato sauce
    8 ounces fresh mushrooms
    2 tablespoons chili powder
    1–2 cayenne peppers, minced
    salt to taste
    cooking oil

Sauté the deerburger, onions, and green peppers in a large skillet with a little cooking oil until the meat is brown and the onions, tender. Add the rest of the ingredients, mix well, and bring to a boil. Reduce the heat, cover, and simmer for 1 hour, stirring from time to time and adding a little liquid if needed. Makes 8 to 10 parsimonious servings—or a meal for 4 hungry hunters.

Ray Arnett's Venison Chili

Here's an interesting recipe, adapted from Cookin' on the Wild Side, *a book published by the Grand National Waterfowl Association. It was contributed by a culinary sport named Ray Arnett of Stockton, California. Where else would you find a venison chili recipe containing carrots, lima beans, and barley?*

    2 pounds venison shoulder
    ¼ pound bacon (preferably on the lean side)
    1 (28-ounce) large can Italian plum tomatoes
    1 (16-ounce) can dark red kidney beans, drained
    3 cups cooked rice or barley (optional)
    2 cups fresh or frozen baby lima beans
    6 medium-sized carrots, chopped
    1 large yellow onion, chopped
    1½ cups beef or chicken stock
    ½ cup red wine
    ¼ cup tomato paste
    2 teaspoons chili powder (or more to taste)
    2 teaspoons ground cumin
    1 teaspoon dried marjoram or oregano
    ¼ teaspoon red pepper flakes (or to taste)

Cut the venison into ½-inch cubes, then cut the bacon into ¼-inch pieces. Cook the bacon in a skillet, stirring as you go, until the pieces are crispy. Remove the bacon with a skimmer and set aside. Measure out 3 tablespoons of bacon drippings. Add 1 tablespoon of the drippings to a skillet, heat, and brown the venison, working in several batches. Set aside. Add the remaining 2 tablespoons of bacon drippings to a stovetop Dutch oven or other suitable pot. Add the onion and carrots. Sprinkle in the chili powder, cumin, marjoram, and red pepper flakes. Cook for about 5 minutes, stirring as you go. Mix in the crisp bacon bits and browned venison along with the tomatoes, beef broth, wine, and tomato paste. Cover and cook at a simmer—do not boil—for 40 minutes. Add the kidney beans and lima beans. Simmer for 10 minutes, stirring as you go with a wooden spoon, tasting and adjusting the spices if needed. Serve hot and plain in bowls, or serve over cooked rice or barley. Feeds 4 to 6.

Variation: Save the crisp bacon bits until the end, then sprinkle over individual servings.

Swampman Dan's Deer Meat Chili

Here's a recipe adapted from Swamp Cookin' with the River People, *by Dana Holyfield. Having only three main ingredients, it's very easy to fix in camp or at home. The water was not included in the recipe, but I have to add some to mine. If you can't find the 7-Alarm Chili Mix, substitute a mix of your choice, or try 6 to 8 tablespoons chili powder spice mix.*

    5 pounds ground deer meat
    3 pounds hamburger meat
    1 (3-ounce) pack 7-Alarm Chili Mix
    water as needed

In a stovetop Dutch oven or other suitable pot, brown the hamburger meat and drain off most of the oil. Add the ground venison and stir in the chili mix. Barely cover with water, bring to a boil, reduce the heat, cover, and simmer for 45 minutes, stirring with a wooden spoon every 5 minutes or so. Serve hot with crackers.

Crock-Pot Chili Con Carne

This recipe calls for both ground and diced meat, which can be provided by elk, moose, or other good game, or a combination of meats.

2 pounds venison, cut into 1-inch cubes
2 pounds venison, ground
¼ pound bulk pork sausage (spicy)
1 (6-ounce) can tomato paste
2 tomato paste cans of water (or 2 cups)
1 medium-to-large onion, diced
3 cloves garlic, minced
4 tablespoons chili powder (or more to taste)
1 tablespoon dark molasses
½ tablespoon freshly ground cumin seeds
1 or more pods of hot red pepper, to taste
salt and black pepper to taste

Mix the meats and put them into the Crock-Pot. Top with the tomato paste and 2 cans of water. Stir in the molasses, pepper, salt, cumin, chili powder, onions, and garlic. Add a pod or two of your favorite hot pepper. Cover tightly, set the heat to low, and forget it for 8 hours. Remove the lid, taste, and add more chili powder, salt, or pepper if needed. Stir, cover, and cook on low for another hour. Serve hot with saltines or tortillas.

Variations: Try topping each bowl of chili with chopped onions, grated cheese, or perhaps a dollop of sour cream, if wanted. If you allow beans in your chili, cook them separately and stir them into each serving bowl.

Pronghorn Chili

Here's a recipe that I have adapted from Captain James A. Smith's book Dress 'em Out. *The pronghorn is often called an antelope, but it's really closer to the goat and the deer. It might well have been a major ingredient of the first Indian chilis of the Southwest. The recipe is short on the amount of chili powder used, and, hence, on the taste of cumin. Add more chili powder, or maybe cumin, if desired.*

1 pound pronghorn meat, cubed or ground
1 pound beef, cubed or ground
1 (16-ounce) can tomato juice
1 (12-ounce) can tomato paste
1 large onion, diced
1 green bell pepper, diced
1 clove garlic, minced
2–3 teaspoons chili powder, or to taste
½ teaspoon cayenne pepper
salt to taste

In a large skillet, brown the meats and onion. Stir in the green pepper and garlic. Reduce the heat, cover, and simmer for a few minutes. Add the chili powder, cayenne, and tomato paste, stirring well. Slowly add the tomato juice and salt. Cover and simmer for 1 hour, or until the pronghorn is as tender as you want it. Feeds 4 to 8.

Venison Chili for LBJ

Lyndon Baines Johnson enjoyed chili on his ranch in Texas as well as in Washington and aboard Air Force One. *This recipe, sometimes called*

Pedernales River Chili, has been reprinted in several publications, sometimes listing beef as the meat. A similar recipe from Lady Bird Johnson also lists beef, but Johnson is said to have preferred venison, possibly on his heart doctor's advice, because it is lower in fat. I like to think that LBJ enjoyed cooking the chili as he lazed away an afternoon down on the ranch, while Lady Bird prepared the tortillas for Noche Specials. But I don't know. Maybe they bought their tortillas ready made. Maybe one of the cooks made the chili, as H. Allen Smith has charged.

    4 pounds venison, coarsely ground
    1½ cups canned tomatoes, chopped
    1 large onion, chopped
    2 cloves garlic, minced
    6 teaspoons chili powder, or more
    1 teaspoon ground oregano
    1 teaspoon cumin seeds
    ⅛ teaspoon hot red pepper sauce, or to taste
    salt to taste
    hot water
    Lady Bird's Noche Specials (chapter 18)

Sear the ground meat in a stovetop Dutch oven and cook it for a few minutes, along with the onions and garlic. Add the rest of the ingredients except for the Noche Specials, using about 2 cups of hot water. Bring to a new boil, lower the heat, cover tightly, and simmer—do not boil—for at least 1 hour. Longer is better, if you've got the time. Stir and add more water from time to time, if needed. Serve with Lady Bird's Noche Specials.

11

CHILI WITH FOWL

Almost all wild and domestic birds can be used to make good chili. Most of the game birds such as quail and grouse are best used in other recipes, but tough pheasant and old wild turkey toms are good choices for chili. The large birds of the ostrich family, including the emu and the rhea, are of especial interest simply because of their size and because they resemble red meat. All of these big birds are available in several cuts and in ground burger form. The meat can be used in any chili recipe that calls for beef.

Although the large ostrich-type birds are becoming more widely available these days, turkey and chicken are still the most widely used birds because of their availability and very affordable price. Because the market ground turkey or chicken is usually a little mushy to suit me, I recommend that you purchase whole birds or parts and either grind or chop the meat at home. Here are a few recipes to try.

Chicken Chili

I confess that I often purchase 10-pound bags of chicken quarters on sale for less than $2. Usually, I cut the drumsticks off and save them for other recipes. The back halves are cut away from the thighs and saved for frying or cooking with rice, or for making chicken and dumplings. The thighs *themselves are skinned and boned (saving the bones for chicken stock). The boned meat is cut into bite-sized chunks and used in this recipe. If you don't want to bother with the large bag of leg quarters, use 10 or 12 chicken thighs. Of course, turkey thighs could also be used.*

>   2–3 pounds boned thigh meat, skin, and fat
>   2 ribs celery with green tops, cut into thin slices
>   1 medium-to-large onion, diced
>   2 cups chicken stock
>   2–3 tablespoons chili powder
>   1 (6-ounce) can tomato paste
>   red pepper flakes to taste
>   salt to taste
>   white rice (cooked separately)

Cut the chicken skins into small pieces and dry them out in a large skillet or stovetop Dutch oven along with the fat, draining and saving the cracklings. Sauté the diced onion, celery, and chicken pieces in the fat rendered from the chicken skins. Stir in the chili powder and tomato paste, along with a little salt and some red pepper flakes. Add the chicken stock, bring to a boil, reduce the heat to very low, cover, and simmer for 1 hour. Stir from time to time and add water if needed. Spoon individual servings of the chili into deep plates or wide soup bowls. Add a dollop of white rice in the middle and sprinkle on a few of the cracklings. Feeds 4 to 6.

Turkey Chili

This recipe can be made with leftover turkey or fresh. I prefer to chop the meat myself, or grind it with a coarse wheel, instead of using a market grind.

2 pounds turkey meat, dark or white
½ pound hard link sausage, such as chorizo
1 (16-ounce) can chopped tomatoes
1 medium-to-large onion, chopped
½ red bell pepper, chopped
½ yellow bell pepper, chopped
1–2 green jalapeño chiles, seeded and chopped
Salt and pepper to taste
2 cups chicken or turkey stock (canned will do)
3 tablespoons chili powder
1 tablespoon bacon drippings or cooking oil
kidney beans, canned or cooked separately

Cut the turkey meat into ½- to ¾-inch chunks. Slice the sausage into ½-inch wheels. In a large skillet or suitable pot, heat the bacon drippings or cooking oil and sauté the sausage wheels for 4 or 5 minutes. Turn and sauté the other side for 2 or 3 minutes. Add the chopped turkey and sprinkle on the chili powder. Cook, stirring a time or two, until the turkey browns lightly. Add the onion, bell peppers, and jalapeño, along with a little salt and freshly ground black pepper. Cook and stir until the onion is clear. Pour in the chicken or turkey stock, along with the canned tomatoes. Bring to a boil, reduce the heat to low, cover tightly, and simmer for an hour or two, stirring from time to time and adding a little water if needed. Add the beans to the pot shortly before serving, or serve on the side as a go–with.

Note: This recipe can also be made with leftover turkey, increasing the measures if need be. Boil the bony parts of the turkey for a couple of hours, along with a little celery and a bay leaf, and use the pot liquid instead of chicken stock.

A. D.'s Bird Gizzard Chili

An Arizona recipe called Angee Scaramuzzo's Lower Colorado Championship Chili was published in the Official Chili Cookbook *a few years ago. It called for all manner of stuff, including some* napalitos en escabeche *from the foothills of the Mohave Mountains. The several kinds of meat included two coots from Lake Havasu. Coots from other locations won't do, the text says. Well, obviously the author never tasted the coots that frequent Orange Lake in Florida, and probably never feasted on the pads of prickly pears that grow along railroads in the Southeast. Anyhow, the author instructs us to boil the coots in seasoned water and beer (neither of which is listed in the ingredients). Later, we are told to add the coot broth to the chili pot, but it isn't clear what to do with the coot meat and frames. In any case, I would advise anyone to skin the coots before proceeding to get rid of some of the fishy taste—especially if you are going to add to the pot ¼ cup of monosodium glutamate, which is said to intensify flavors.*

I think it's better to use the coot frames in another recipe designed to use with fish-eating ducks and save the gizzards for the chili. As Marjorie Kinnan Rawlings knew, coots have a very large gizzard that is as good as or better than a chicken gizzard. Turkey and pheasant gizzards can also be used, along with the much smaller ones from quail and doves. All of these gizzards should be properly dressed and cut into ½-inch pieces. (To dress a gizzard, slit it from one side to the other, turn it inside out, and discard the digest. Wash and dice as usual.) Note also that the bird hearts can be used along with the gizzards. Both will stand up to long, slow simmering.

If you don't have coots or other birds, note that you can purchase packaged chicken gizzards at the grocery store at very reasonable cost. These will be dressed and ready to dice, and may contain some chicken hearts. In any case, here's my basic recipe.

2 pounds bird gizzards and hearts, diced
¼ pound salt pork, diced
1 (16-ounce) can tomatoes
3 tablespoons chili powder, or to taste
2 tablespoons diced cactus pad (optional)
1 large onion, diced
1 stalk celery, diced
salt and black pepper to taste

Try out the salt pork in a large skillet or suitable pot. Brown the onion lightly. Add the diced gizzards and sauté for a few minutes. Add the rest of the ingredients, using enough water to barely cover the meat. Simmer for several hours, or until the meat is very tender. Stir from time to time and add more water, as needed. Serve over rice or noodles.

Note: Bird gizzards and hearts are a rich, lean, very dark meat. If you want a white chili, use mullet gizzards. These are usually fried in Florida, but can be cooked in a number of ways and have been prized in the cuisines of other lands, especially around the Mediterranean. The French once called the mullet the woodcock of the sea because of its innards. In any case, mullet gizzards are perfectly white and have a very mild flavor—not at all fishy. For a two-toned chili, why not combine coot and mullet gizzards?

12

CHILI WITH . . . WHAT-YA-GOT?

Lamb makes good chili, although it is not widely used in America. Some supermarkets sell ground lamb, but it's really best to buy a whole shoulder, bone out the meat, and dice it. Use the bone for making a stock. If you want to take the trouble, cook down some lamb shanks, bone out the meat, and make a stock from the bones.

Goat is used for chili in parts of Texas and a few hot spots here and there, but it is not widely available in most parts of the country. This is slowly changing, however, as ethnic groups and good ol' boys are looking for the meat. More and more people are raising dairy goats for meat and milk. I'm not offering a goat recipe here, but I wouldn't hesitate to use goat shoulder, either ground or diced, for any chili recipe calling for venison.

The American buffalo, or bison, is a purely excellent choice for making chili. These are raised commercially these days and the meat is available in some markets, and by mail order. Use bison in any chili recipe that calls for beef. The real buffalo (African Cape buffalo and water buffalo) are also edible and will no doubt make good chili, but they are not readily available in America. Not yet. There has been some experimentation with raising water buffalo in the low country in and around the Florida Everglades, but most such endeavors usually play out short of reaching supermarket status. Still, chiliheads who enjoy exotic meats should make an effort to obtain these.

Clearly, almost any good meat can be used in chili, including unusual or exotic fare ranging from armadillo to zebra. Here are a few recipes to try.

Rattlesnake Chili

It's not unusual to see chili recipes, usually from bodacious Texans and good ol' boys, that call for rattlesnake. Some people do indeed eat rattlesnakes at every opportunity, and I am one of these. Be warned, however, that a rattlesnake is lean and usually tough, and contains very little meat. What meat there is, is difficult to bone because the snake is mostly skin and backbone from head to tail. Rattlesnake meat can be purchased by mail order from firms specializing in exotic meats; I have seen whole snake listed, along with boned meat. Canned rattlesnake is also available. If you want to substitute chicken or turkey, you should try the meat off the necks.

2 pounds fresh pork, cut into ½-inch cubes
1 pound boned rattlesnake meat, cut into ¼-inch cubes
1 quart chicken broth or stock
2 large onions, chopped
6 cloves garlic, chopped
½ cup stone-ground white cornmeal
¼ cup chili powder (with spices and cumin)
¼ cup peanut oil
½ tablespoon Mexican oregano
salt and freshly ground black pepper to taste
Tabasco or other hot sauce

Pour some Tabasco over the rattlesnake and pork and let stand for a few minutes. Heat the peanut oil in a skillet. Brown the meats a little at a time. Set aside to drain. Add more oil to the skillet if needed, then sauté the onions and garlic for 5 or 6 minutes, stirring with a wooden spoon as you go. Add the meat, onions, garlic, chili powder, salt, a little black pepper, and oregano to a stovetop Dutch oven or other suitable pot. Add the broth or stock. Bring to a boil. Sprinkle on and stir in a little of the cornmeal, using a wooden spoon. Reduce the heat to low and stir in the rest of the cornmeal a little at a time, cover, and simmer for 2 or 3 hours, stirring from time to time, tasting and adding more water, salt, or pepper if needed. Serve hot in bowls with crackers and rattlesnake beans on the side.

Outback Chilli with Two L's

A culinary melting pot, Australia has drawn from the cuisines of East and West. The American chile pepper (usually spelled "chilli" with two l's) fits right in, and, with it, chilli con carne. In recent years upscale cooks have been taking a look at native Australian cookery, using such exotic meats as kangaroo and emu and crocodile. Other outback meats include rabbits (introduced from Europe), buffalo, and, of all things, feral camel (introduced from Africa or Asia). This recipe, adapted from Australia: The Beautiful Cookbook, *called for venison, but it works well with any good red meat. The use of only 1 teaspoon of dried small red chile peppers indicates that this ingredient is generally considered a spice, not a vegetable, contributing only heat and not much in the way of nutrition or texture. The recipe would be improved with a generous helping of chile powder.*

1 pound ground outback meat
1 large (28-ounce) can Roma tomatoes
1 large (28-ounce) can red kidney beans, drained
2 stalks celery, chopped

2 brown onions, chopped
4 cloves garlic, crushed
1¼ cups beef stock (or other stock)
¼ cup olive oil
2 tablespoons tomato paste
1 tablespoon ground cumin
1 teaspoon dried small chile peppers
1 teaspoon cocoa powder
½ teaspoon dried oregano
½ teaspoon ground allspice
salt to taste

Heat the oil in a saucepan and sauté the onions for a few minutes, until they start to brown. Add the celery and garlic, cooking for 4 or 5 minutes. Stir in the ground meat and cook, stirring as you go, until it is lightly browned with no lumps. Add the tomatoes, the juice from the can, tomato paste, stock, and the rest of the ingredients except for the beans. Bring to a light boil, reduce the heat to very low, and cook—uncovered—for 1¼ hours. (Stir from time to time and add a little water if needed.) Add the beans and simmer for 20 to 30 minutes. Serve hot in bowls, with sour cream on the side, if wanted. The Aussie book says the recipe will serve 6, but I say 2 to 4. The book also says that the dish is worth making several days ahead, to allow the flavors to develop. I agree.

Justin Wilson's Crawfish Chili

Here's a recipe from the late Justin Wilson, the professional Cajun, who apparently suffered no compunctions about mixing white wine, crawfish tail, and, of all things, a little green mint in a pot of red.

2 pounds chili-grind beef
2 pounds peeled crawfish tails
1 (8-ounce) can tomato sauce
1 cup chopped onions
1 cup dry white wine
3 tablespoons chili powder
1 tablespoon soy sauce
1 tablespoon dried parsley
2 teaspoons salt
1 teaspoon dried mint
1 teaspoon cayenne pepper
1 teaspoon garlic, minced
1 teaspoon lemon or lime juice
bacon drippings
water

In a stovetop Dutch oven or other suitable pot, brown the beef in some bacon drippings. Mix in all the other ingredients, adding just enough water to cover. Bring to a boil, cover tightly, reduce the heat to very low, and simmer for a few hours. Stir from time to time and add more water if needed. Serve hot in bowls.

Javelina Green Chili

Green chili seems to be especially popular in the Southwest, where the peppers grow and the javelina roams. If you are lucky enough to get a good shoat, make this chili from shoulder meat. Wild or domestic pig will also work, as will any sort of green peppers. I would suggest jalapeño or a mix of hot and mild peppers.

2 pounds javelina or pork, cut into bites
20 green peppers, hot or mild, as you like it
3 cups chopped tomatoes
2 medium-to-large onions, chopped
4 cloves garlic, minced
¼ cup chopped fresh chives or green onion tops
2 tablespoons sunflower seed oil
1 teaspoon cumin seeds, crushed
salt to taste
water as needed

Roast the green chile peppers on a grill or stovetop burner until blackened, turning as needed. Put the peppers into a bag for a few minutes. Then peel, seed, and trim the peppers. Cut them into slices about 1 inch wide. Heat the oil in a stovetop Dutch oven or other suitable pot. Add the javelina or pork and cook until lightly browned, stirring a time or two with a wooden spoon. Add the rest of the ingredients, using just enough water to cover. Bring to a light boil, reduce the heat to very low, cover, and simmer for an hour or longer, until the meat is very tender. If long cooking is required for tough meat, be sure to stir from time to time and add more water as needed.

Variation: If you want red chili instead of green, use large dried red peppers, such an ancho or New Mexico, and a little more cumin.

Muskrat Chili

The muskrat (a clean vegetarian that lives for the most part in the water) was once an important source of food in some areas. It can still be seen in markets and on menus from Louisiana to Chesapeake Bay, up into Canada, and over to Alaska. This unusual dish, adapted here from Cooking Alaskan, *can also be cooked with fox or gray squirrel, using about 3 pounds of dressed meat. The muskrats or squirrels are cut into serving-sized pieces. If you are feeding squeamish folk, you might consider calling the muskrat "marsh rabbit." That's what the Cajuns do. If that doesn't help, try putting lots of cayenne into the recipe and double up on the wine.*

3 yearling muskrats, dressed and cut up
¼ cup red wine
⅓ cup chili sauce
2 tablespoons brown sugar
1 teaspoon dehydrated minced onion
½ teaspoon chili powder
½ teaspoon dry mustard
½ teaspoon Worcestershire sauce
salt and black pepper to taste

Sprinkle the meat pieces with a little salt and fit them into a Crock-Pot. Mix the rest of the ingredients in a bowl and pour over the meat. Cover and cook on low heat for 8 hours or more. Serve hot with crackers or sourdough bread.

Note: If you have a yearling nutria—another edible water rodent that is now plentiful in some coastal areas of the South—be sure to try it instead of muskrat.

Conch Chili

I found this believe-it-or-not recipe in Chili Cookbook, *a small work published by the St. George Island Chili Cook-off in Florida. Conch is a tough white meat that stands up to long simmering. If you don't have conch, try any similar meat such as abalone or perhaps squid or octopus. Also try it with mullet gizzards, which also have a very tough, quite white, and surprisingly mild meat. Note that the amount of chile in the recipe, available only in 1 to 2 teaspoons chili powder, is on the scant side, although the chipotle peppers help.*

1½ pounds conch, ground
1 (14½-ounce) can great northern beans, drained
1 (14½-ounce) can diced tomatoes
1 (6-ounce) can chipotle peppers
2 cups tomato juice
1 cup beer
1 green bell pepper, minced
1 onion, minced
4 toes garlic, minced
2 tablespoons olive oil
2 tablespoons lime juice
1 tablespoon Worcestershire sauce
2 teaspoons ground oregano
2 teaspoons ground cumin
1–2 teaspoons chili powder
1 teaspoon red hot sauce
2 bay leaves
salt and black pepper to taste
scallops for garnish (cooked separately)

Chop the chipotle peppers and set aside, along with the juices. Heat the olive oil in a skillet and sauté the onion, bell pepper, garlic, and oregano for 4 or 5 minutes, stirring as you go with a wooden spoon. Add the conch meat, diced tomatoes, tomato juice, beer, chipotle peppers and reserved liquid, chili powder, cumin, Worcestershire, hot sauce, salt, black pepper, and bay leaves. Simmer on low heat for 30 minutes, stirring a time or two. Add the beans and lime juice. Cover and simmer until the conch is tender and the liquids are almost absorbed. Serve hot in bowls, topped with scallops.

Note: The recipe calls for chopped scallops, but I think the small calico bay scallops served whole are much the better choice. I like them sautéed lightly in butter with a little lime juice. True Conchs, as the older residents of the Florida Keys are called, might well prefer to serve fresh scallops raw.

Osmose Zoo Chili

My friend and culinary sport Greg Rane came up with this seven-meat recipe when representing his company, Great Southern Wood Preserving, in a chili cook-off. I first used the recipe in my Complete Fish & Game Cookbook, *published a few years back, and reprint it here because it's a fun recipe to cook and fun to eat and fun to know.*

GROUP ONE

5 pounds lean ground beef
1 pound deer tenderloin, cubed small
1 pound mild pan sausage
10 ounces chicken (white meat)
10 ounces shark (preferably from just behind dorsal fin)
6 ounces rabbit
6 ounces squirrel

GROUP TWO

3 large onions, chopped
4 chili peppers, punctured several times with fork
2 large green peppers, chopped
2 large jalapeño peppers, chopped
1 jar of peperoncini peppers, chopped

GROUP THREE

1 large can chili powder (add to taste)
3 tablespoons sugar
3 to 5 teaspoons cumin powder (add to taste)
2 teaspoons salt
black pepper to taste (approximately 1 tablespoon)
1 teaspoon MSG (monosodium glutamate)

GROUP FOUR

2 (14-ounce) cans tomatoes
3 (10-ounce) cans tomato puree
1 (10-ounce) can tomato paste
2 cans Budweiser beer
1 small jar lemon-pepper spice
1 lemon
½ stick butter

Rane says:

Pour tomato products into a large pot (approximately 3 or 4 gallon). Be sure to squash tomatoes with your hands. Cook on low for 1 hour, stirring frequently and making sure not to burn. Add ingredients from group three. Stir in and mix. Cover and simmer.

Lightly sauté onions and all the peppers in group two. Add to pot. Brown hamburger, sausage, and deer meat. Drain off, add to pot, and stir in. Chop rabbit, squirrel, and chicken. Sauté and add to pot. Stir in.

Melt butter, then add lemon-pepper and lemon juice. Sauté shark. When it is cooked, flake it and stir it into the pot. Cook on low slowly for at least 2 hours, stirring frequently.

As chili cooks down and consistency thickens NEVER ADD WATER! Add beer as needed to suit thickness. The longer this chili cooks, the better it gets. Enjoy.

13

JERKY CHILI FOR CAMP OR TRAIL

These days most Americans consider jerky to be noshing fare, a good chew, a high-energy snack, or perhaps a compact food for distance runners, backpackers, and mountain climbers. Originally, jerky had a more everyday purpose. Before canning techniques and mechanical refrigeration were perfected, most of our meats were cured by drying. Making jerky was the primary way to preserve meats for long periods of time.

The jerky always made a good raw chew, but usually it was cooked in soups and stews. Often it was soaked overnight in water to reconstitute it, but this step is not necessary if long, slow cooking is practical. Even today in South America, *charqui* or dried beef is frequently used in soups and stews of national importance, and on the pampas of Argentina dried rhea or guanaco fills in nicely. Usually, the charqui is mixed in with several other meats, including pig's feet, and stewed down in a large pot. In some other parts of Latin America, dried meat is called *seca*. It's all jerky.

The modern method of cutting jerky into thin strips makes the meat easier to dry, but larger chunks and slabs can be jerked successfully, and these really contain more flavor. Usually, the jerking process starts with lots of salt being sprinkled onto the raw meat to draw out the moisture and help preserve the meat. I do not make jerky without white salt. With one exception. For thin strips,

I often marinate the meat for several hours in regular soy sauce (not the "lite" or low-sodium kind). Then I dry it without additional salt, although I might sprinkle it with freshly ground black pepper. But remember that full-strength soy sauce is quite salty.

Although thin strips of meat are easy to dry and handy for chewing, I think that chunks of meat are much better for cooking. I call these jerky nuggets. Various methods and many recipes for making jerky are covered in my book *Jerky,* from which part of this chapter has been painfully extracted, but for cooking purposes you really don't need to flavor the meat very much. I like to sprinkle it with salt and dry it in a dehydrator at 120°F for several hours, or until dry to my liking. These modern electrically heated dehydrators make it easier to make jerky, and vacuum-pack systems make long storage almost foolproof.

Strips of jerky can be cut into pieces for soups and stews—but nuggets, after many hours of simmering, make the best imaginable chili. Pemmican, a mixture of powdered jerky and fat, can be used for quick chili and will be discussed in a recipe later in this chapter. Meanwhile, cut up a sirloin tip, jerk it, and try the recipes below, or use the jerky in any recipe that calls for long simmering.

Jerky-Style Camp Chili

Here's an easy recipe for camp cooking, made to taste without having to measure the ingredients. If you've got some wild onions near camp, be sure to chop a few of these, along part of their green tops, and add them to your chili during the cooking phase.

    beef jerky in strips
    chili powder to taste
    wild onions (optional)

salt
water

Cut the jerky strips into 1-inch pieces. Cover with water in a pot, bring to a boil, reduce the heat to simmer, and cook on very low heat for 2 or 3 hours. As it cooks the jerky will absorb liquid, so be sure to add more water as needed. Stir from time to time, taste, and add some chili powder and salt. If you have wild onions or ramps free for the pulling, finely chop a few, including part of the green tops, and throw into the pot, remembering that some wild onions and garlic are quite strong. Stir, taste, and simmer until you have it right. Serve with rice or beans. Mix it all together if you like. If you don't have much jerky and need to feed lots of people, add some rice to the pot during the last 30 minutes of cooking.

A. D.'s Jerky Chili

For this recipe it's best to use a mild, basic jerky, which can be made with beef, venison, ostrich, and other good meats. If the jerky is highly spiced, however, you might want to modify the recipe ingredients accordingly. In any case, this is an excellent chili for cooking in camp.

½ pound basic jerky
¼ cup cooking oil
2–3 tablespoons prepared chili powder
1 tablespoon red pepper flakes (or to taste)
1 tablespoon dried onion flakes
1 teaspoon garlic powder
1 teaspoon cumin seeds, crushed
water
flour or fine cornmeal (if needed)

Cut the strips of jerky into ½-inch pieces. Heat the oil in a cast-iron pot. Add the jerky pieces and stir for a few minutes. Add the chili powder and stir until well mixed. Stir in the rest of the seasonings and cover well with water. Bring to a boil, reduce the heat to very low, and simmer (do not boil) for 3 hours, stirring from time to time and adding more water as needed. Cool the chili, then reheat it for serving. Thicken with a little paste made with flour and water, if needed. Serve hot in bowls, adding beans, chopped onions, and other toppings, if wanted. Corn pone or rolled tortillas go nicely with this chili, but saltines will do. Feeds 2 to 4.

Note: For camp cookery, consider mixing all the spices, chili powder, and flavorings at home and taking them afield in a plastic zip bag or small jar.

Chile Con Seca

If you use jerky strips for this recipe, snip them into 1-inch pieces with poultry shears. This is a recipe for stirring and tasting, adjusting the seasonings as you go. Make sure you have lots of time, preferably on a cold day.

    2 or 3 pounds dried beef
    4 strips bacon
    4 tablespoons commercial chili powder
    cumin seeds (use sparingly)
    tomato paste (optional)
    red pepper flakes
    salt
    boiling water
    beans or rice (cooked separately)
    chopped spring onions, if wanted

Cut the dried beef into pieces of about ½ inch. Fry the bacon in a stovetop Dutch oven. Drain and crumble the bacon, saving it for later use. Put the jerky into the pot and cook in the bacon drippings for a few minutes, stirring as you go. Cover with boiling water. Bring to a new boil, stirring in a little of the chili powder, cumin seeds, salt, red pepper flakes, and tomato paste. Cover and simmer—do not boil—for several hours, or until the meat is very tender. Be sure to add more water as needed and stir from time to time with a wooden spoon or wooden spatula, scraping up any bottom dredgings. After the first hour of cooking, add more chili powder, red pepper flakes, salt, or tomato paste, whichever is needed to suit your taste. Serve hot in large bowls, adding a dollop of beans or rice in the middle. Top with bacon bits and chopped spring onions, if wanted. Have plenty of crackers on the side, or perhaps soft cornmeal tortillas rolled for easy sopping.

Chili Con Carne from Pemmican

Here's an idea from George Leonard Herter, connected to the old Herter mail enterprise, who seems to have been somewhat haunted by fears of the atomic bomb back in the 1950s. Pemmican was once sold commercially and became an important item of trade for the Native Americans and European settlers. It was usually sold in slabs of 80 or 90 pounds. Later, in the Southwest, chili bricks were made and sold in the same manner, making use of lots of chile pulp and animal fat. Like pemmican, the chile brick was especially suitable for journey food during the western expansion. A little boiling water turned the bricks into quick chili.

Start by making the pemmican, which is a combination of powdered jerky and dried fruit with melted animal fat mixed in.

CHILI

2 pounds jerky, finely ground or powdered
½ pound dried fruit, finely ground
¼ cup sugar
10 ounces melted beef suet

Mix the dry ingredients and stir in the suet. Shape into blocks or small loaves and store in glass jars until needed. (Some people dip the blocks into melted paraffin. Modern practitioners can profit by storing the loaves in jars or plastic bags with one of the vacuum-pack systems.) Keep in a cool place until needed.

To make chili, possibly in camp, put the pemmican into a little boiling water and stir in some chili powder. Boil for a few minutes, then serve hot. Beans can also be added, if wanted.

Variation: The recipe given here makes a sort of all-purpose pemmican, which can be eaten raw or cooked. If you want the pemmican especially for chili, omit the dried fruit and sugar. Add a little cornmeal or flour for nutrition and texture. On the trail or during a Herter-inspired drill for an atomic bomb attack, a few ground mesquite beans or sweet acorns will tighten the chili nicely.

PART THREE

Bodacious Chili and Bragging Rights

Braggadocio is an important part of the chili tradition, and I trust that chapters 14 and 15 can help carry the banter.

Chapter 16, on more serious ground, contains some thoughts on different kinds of chili based on regional or cultural institutions. The section on family cookbook recipes, past and present, should be especially interesting to chiliheads and to anyone interested in the development of American cooking and foods.

14

CHILI WITH ATTITUDES

Charles Pendergast, a Texas newspaperman, argued that the best chili is made from very tough beef. He wasn't talking about the tougher supermarket cuts, either, all neatly cut and wrapped in clear plastic. What he had in mind was more like an old Texas long-horn range cow. In fact, the ingredients list for one of his recipes calls for 5 pounds of "lean muscle meat from an animal of maturity and character."

Clearly, Pendergast had firm opinions, expressed them well, and felt no compunction to be politically correct. Here are a few other staunchly defended points of view and highly denounced pet peeves regarding chili, along with interesting recipes.

Chili According to Mel Marshall

In his Complete Book of Outdoor Cookery, *Mel Marshall said, "There's nothing better than good camp-cooked chili, and sadly there's no dish which has undergone more wanton tinkering than has chili con carne. . . . There isn't space enough here for me to list all the reasons why most of the alterations to chili are phony, so please take my word that tomatoes, paprika, sour cream, lime juice, ketchup, red wine, Tabasco Sauce, soy sauce, butter, or beans of any kind but especially kidney beans have no place whatever in chili con carne." Marshall gives in just a little, however, allowing beans to be cooked and served separately, "so long as they're pinto beans."*

Like Pendergast, Marshall advises us to use the least desirable, leanest, and toughest beef that we can find.

4 pounds tough beef flank, shank, or arm meat
¼–½ pound beef suet
1½ cups chopped onion
2 cloves garlic, minced
2 tablespoons ground chile
1½ teaspoons cumin seeds
1½ teaspoons salt
water

Grind the cumin seeds with a mortar and pestle, then mix in the salt and chili powder. Dice the beef suet into ½-inch pieces and try them out in a stovetop Dutch oven. Remove the cracklings, leaving the hot fat in the pot. Add the chopped beef to the pan a handful at a time, stirring in a little of the spice mix as you go. When the beef is seared nicely, drain it and pour out most of the fat. Sauté the onion and garlic in the pot until lightly browned. Add the seared beef, stir, and pour in enough water to cover the meat by 1 inch. Simmer on low heat—but do not boil—for 1 to 1½ hours, adding more water from time to time if needed. Feeds 6 to 8.

CHILI ACCORDING TO ED MARTLEY

From Texas to Alaska we quickly go. Here's a recipe quoted verbatim from the book *Cooking Alaskan,* which, in turn, credited Ed Martley, *Fairbanks Daily News-Miner.* There are several points of opinion in this recipe, such as the necessity of celery as an ingredient, but it's the overall tone of the prose that catches the spirit of the chili, although, in my opinion, the short, choppy paragraphs have been too much influenced by newspaper style of writing. Still, in spite of the jerky text, the recipe seems to fit very well into this book, once one accepts the fact that chili put together with short paragraphs can be not only palatable but downright good. Anyhow, here is Martley's best:

> One of the finest things to find on the table after coming in from the cold is a steaming bowl of chili.
>
> And one of the finest ingredients in chili is game meat—moose, caribou, rabbit—anything.
>
> Chili is not made from a recipe. It's made from one's heart, and therein lies the secret of its great popularity. It's never the same and the flavor of each batch depends on the mood you're in while you make it.
>
> We'll give you the ingredients—try not to vary from them—but juggle the proportions to your own taste.
>
> Start with a large kettle, capable of holding slightly more than a gallon (3.8 L). Brown several pounds (1 kg or more) of stew meat in the bottom. (Caribou is fantastic.)
>
> During the browning procedure, start adding other ingredients. Load it down with chopped onion—don't be afraid to get too much as it will eventually cook away, leaving only a subtle flavor. For a gallon (3.8 L) of chili (and there's no point in making less) use at least two large onions.
>
> The secret ingredient for making an unforgettable chili is celery. De-string and chop about half as much celery as you have onion. Celery will give the final product an unidentifiable but marvelous flavor which

makes this chili stand head and shoulders above other types. Throw the celery in with the browning meat.

Next comes seasoning. Use chili powder, garlic salt, cayenne pepper, if you wish, and salt and pepper. This is where a good taste sense will help you. Add the seasoning gradually, tasting as you go. When it's seasoned just a little too strong to be easily eatable, you have it just right. You see, the other ingredients you are to add will dilute the strong spices.

Next comes the liquid—by adding canned tomatoes and tomato soup (use both), make it just a little thinner than you want it to be when you eat it. It will boil down during cooking.

Now, add some canned kidney beans. Put in as many as you like but don't go overboard. Navy beans would be okay except their pale color is a bit repulsive to some.

Simmer the whole mess for a long, long time. The celery is the best indicator of when it's ready to eat. Put the chili in bowl when the celery is very soft and not before then. Serve with saltine crackers spread with butter. Have some cayenne pepper on the table so those who like it hot can add their own.

The more often chili is reheated, the better it is. And nothing freezes better—pour it into half-gallon (1.9 L) milk cartons.

Chances are you may be tempted to gunk up your chili with other ingredients. Don't. The above items all have their own distinct flavors which are very complimentary to one another.

Mexican Chili According to George C. Booth

The author of The Food and Drink of Mexico, *George C. Booth says that cooking good chili is like making a good marriage. You must, he explains, give the same narrow-eyed scrutiny to finding the right type of bean that you would to choosing a wife. He recommends the Mexican red bean. The bay bean is second, he says—with the pinto coming in third. (That ought to rile the Texans.) Booth is fussy in other regards also, saying, for example, to be careful about when you add the salt to the pot. Anyhow, here's what you'll need.*

    2 pounds lean stew beef
    1 pound dry beans
    5 medium-to-large tomatoes, chopped
    2 large onions, sliced
    1 clove garlic, minced
    2 bay leaves
    2 tablespoons bacon drippings or vegetable oil
    2 tablespoons salt (added late)
    2 tablespoons cornmeal
    1½ tablespoons black pepper
    1 tablespoon chili powder (or to taste)
    ¼ teaspoon dried oregano, powdered
    ¼ teaspoon dried sage, powdered
    ¼ teaspoon dried cumin, powdered

Have your woman pick over the beans for trash and soak overnight in cool water, Booth says. The next morning, put the beans into a pot, cover with water, and bring to a boil. Add the bay leaves, onions, and garlic. (Hold the salt.) Cover and simmer until the beans are tender. Heat the bacon drippings in a skillet and brown the stew beef. Add the tomatoes, cornmeal, and all the remaining spices, including the salt. Cook for 5 minutes, stirring as you go. Add to the main pot, cover, and simmer for another hour. Feeds 8.

Note: Booth claims that adding the salt too soon will harden the beans, as the Aztecs, he adds, knew a thousand years ago. This has been disputed in modern times, however, as has the practice of soaking the beans overnight.

Chili According to H. Allen Smith

A humorist and culinary rabble-rouser by the name of H. Allen Smith once wrote that Texans don't know how to make good chili. Although his articles on the subject succeeded in riling up the Texans and fanned the flames of the chili cook-offs down in Terlingua, and probably helped spur the Texas legislature into declaring chili to be the official state food, it turns out that Smith didn't know how to make a good bowl of red either. His final recipe called for beans and tomato, each of which, and sometimes both, are scorned by some purists. Anyhow, this recipe, sometimes billed as "H. Allen Smith's Perfect Chili," is the humorist's last published word on the subject. I, for one, am grateful for a little black pepper in the recipe, with rights to adjust the seasonings as needed toward the end. I suspect, however, that the scant ½ teaspoon of basil went in just to stir up trouble.

4 pounds sirloin or tenderloin tips, coarsely ground
1–2 cans of pinto or pink beans (can size not specified)
1–2 (6-ounce) cans tomato paste
1 quart water
3–4 medium onions, chopped
1 large bell pepper, chopped
2–10 cloves garlic, minced
olive oil or butter, or both

3 tablespoons chili powder, or more
1 tablespoon cumin seeds or ground cumin
1 tablespoon oregano
½ teaspoon basil
salt and black pepper to taste

Using a stovetop Dutch oven or other suitable pot, cook the meat in a little olive oil or butter for a few minutes, until it is nicely gray but not quite brown. Add the tomato paste and water, using some of the water to flush out the can. Stir well and add the rest of the ingredients except for the canned beans. Cover tightly and simmer for 2 or 3 hours, stirring occasionally and adding a little water if needed. Taste and correct the seasonings. Add the beans and cook for 15 minutes. Serve hot.

Note: I've seen another recipe by H. Allen Smith, in which he called for ground chuck. Smith also has firm opinions about what should not be in chili. In one article, he says he renounced his vote for LBJ in 1964 because of his evil ways with chili. Johnson, you see, allowed an old ranch cook to thicken the chili with cracker meal, whereas Smith preferred a thin chili without thickeners. Another of Johnson's cooks served the chili without beans, Smith goes on, astoundedly.

In a widely distributed chili recipe released after Smith's comments, Johnson's recipe did not even mention cracker meal or any other tightener. He didn't take a stand on beans, either. Was he being politically correct, even with the state dish of Texas at stake?

A. D.'s Basic Chili with Jalapeño Corndodgers

I don't fully understand why H. Allen Smith disallowed cornmeal in chili, but I suspect the poor fellow never tasted the right stuff. Many other people think of cornmeal as an odd ingredient for chili—including some who do not realize that they have been using it all along in their favorite chili mixes, sometimes under the name of masa harina. Most of this stuff is dry, gritty, tasteless, and not very nutritious as compared with fresh stone-ground cornmeal. The fresher the better, and culinary sports ought to look into grinding their own cornmeal with one of the new and inexpensive kitchen mills, for the same reason they ought to grind their own coffee and black pepper.

Just stay away from supermarket cornmeal, unless you can find genuine and reasonably fresh stone-ground meal (which is sometimes available in some areas of the South and Rhode Island, thank God). As I have said in The Whole Grain Cookbook, the gritty yellow cornmeal sold in supermarkets these days is unfit for human consumption. My dog Nosher won't even eat chili or hush puppies made with the stuff. (How's that for attitude?)

4 pounds ground chuck
4–5 strips smoked bacon
2 cups stone-ground cornmeal (very fresh)
½ cup ancho or New Mexico chile powder
1 large onion, chopped
1 small red jalapeño
1 small green jalapeño
1 tablespoon cumin seeds, powdered
hot red pepper flakes to taste
1 teaspoon salt, plus more to taste
water as needed

In a cast–iron stovetop Dutch oven, cook the bacon until crisp. Set it aside to drain. In the drippings, cook the ground meat until it is gray, stirring often to break up the clumps of meat. Add the onions and cook a few minutes longer, stirring in the chili powder, salt, red pepper flakes, and cumin seeds as you go. Add enough water to cover the chili, bearing in mind that you will want a rather thin gravy. Cover the pot and cook at a bare simmer for 2 hours or longer, stirring and adding more water as needed. About 45 minutes before serving time, seed and mince the red and green jalapeño peppers. Put the cornmeal into a suitable bowl and stir in a little water, just barely enough to make a dough. Crumble the bacon and stir it into the dough, along with most or part of the jalapeño, depending on whether you want hot or mild corndodgers. Let this sit for about 30 minutes at room temperature, allowing it to thicken and set. Do not stir the chili during this time period. Now take the lid off the pot and, using a large spoon, skim off some of that wonderful red oil that will have accumulated on top. Stir some of the oil into the cornmeal dough, mixing it well until you have a drop-dumpling consistency. (Without the oil or meat stock of some kind, the corndodgers could well cook apart in the bowl of red—and be warned that commercial cornmeal is even more likely to cook apart. If in doubt, proceed slowly and carefully.)

Wet a tablespoon in water, then carefully spoon a blob of the cornmeal dough into the pot. Do not stir, which would tend to break up the cornmeal dough. Carefully add another spoonful and another until you have a dozen or so corndodgers floating on top. Do not overcrowd. (If you have dough left over, fry it like hush puppies to serve with the chili.) Stir the chili carefully and watch it closely as you simmer for about 15 minutes. A little of the cornmeal should have cooked off the dodgers—not too much but just enough to thicken the chili to your liking. If the gravy isn't thick enough, keep cooking and slowly stirring until you get it right. If the corndodgers disintegrate and make a thickened mess out of the chili, throw it all out and start over. When you get it right, serve hot, carefully floating two white corndodgers in each bowl of red.

Chili Mary of Agreda (#2), According to Herter

In the book called Bull Cook and Authentic Historical Recipes and Practices, *George Leonard Herter goes on at some length about the quality of Spanish cooks in general, their having been influenced at one time or another by hordes of Phoenicians, Greeks, Romans, Moors, and Arabs, and of Basque cooks in particular. When the Spanish came to America, they, of course, had an influence on the native cookery. According to Herter, the recipe for chili was given to the Native Americans of the Southwest by Mary of Agreda, an early missionary nun (Herter says) to what is now Texas, New Mexico, Arizona, and Southern California. Of course, the Native Americans already had meat and chile peppers. What the Spanish brought was cumin, called* comino, *and other spices, along with beef and pork and other ingredients. Anyhow, printed below is Sister Mary's "original" and authentic recipe, according to Herter.*

As pointed out in chapter 1, however, other sources say that Mary of Agreda never visited the Americas in the flesh, but did experience some sort of out-of-body experience—and that she received the recipe from the Native Americans, not the other way around. Well . . . maybe she received the recipe for basic chili set forth in chapter 1 by an out-of-body experience to the New World, worked on it in Spain, added some European spices, and sent the following recipe back to the Native Americans and Spanish settlers on a return trip. How, exactly, Herter got hold of the "authentic historical" recipe is an untold miracle.

2 pounds beef, mutton, venison, or antelope
1 pound pork (the original was wild javelina, Herter says)
1 quart ripe tomatoes
1 medium-to-large onion, minced
4 cloves garlic
1 cup chile pepper pulp

2 tablespoons lard, beef suet, or antelope fat
3 bay leaves
1 level tablespoon oregano
1 level tablespoon salt
1 level teaspoon ground cumin
red pepper (powdered cayenne), if needed
red beans (cooked separately)
water

Cube the meats into bite-sized pieces, about 1 inch square. Heat the fat in a stovetop Dutch oven or other suitable pot. Sauté the onion and garlic for 3 or 4 minutes. Add the cubed meat along with 3 "level" tablespoons of water. Cover and let steam for 5 minutes. Mash the tomatoes through a colander, adding them to the pot along with the chile pepper pulp, oregano, salt, bay leaves, and cumin. Cover tightly and cook slowly (simmer, do not boil) for about 2 hours, stirring from time to time and adding a little water as needed to prevent scorching the bottom. Also add a little cayenne if you want a hotter bowl of red.

Herter says to serve the hot chili over cooked beans. Never cook the beans with the chili. If you do, he says, you will end up with a "sticky mess of nothing that does not even resemble Chile-Con-Carne." This statement is, of course, in direct conflict with H. Allen Smith and other champions of the bean.

Although his recipes on historical principle may be open to question and in spite of Herter's need for everything he sets forth to be "authentic," I think his recipe is right on the money, culinarily speaking, partly because it contains quite a bit of pulp from dried red chile peppers along with the cumin. It might well be the world's best modern chili recipe, if it is made with tender loving care. Could the guy, after all, have been inspired?

Marine Chili According to Walter McIlhenny

The McIlhenny family of Tabasco Sauce fame have ruled Avery Island, Louisiana, for four generations. Edmund McIlhenny started it all not long after the Civil War. Somewhere along the way Walter McIlhenny became an important boss in the company. He was a jackleg chef who liked to entertain on the island, where this chili was sometimes served to marine guests.

3 pounds lean beef
1 cup chopped onions
3 cloves garlic, minced
1 (4-ounce) can chopped green chiles
¼ cup vegetable oil
3 tablespoons chili powder
2 teaspoons ground cumin
2 teaspoons salt
2 teaspoons Tabasco Sauce
3 cups water
rice (cooked separately)
chopped onions (garnish)
shredded cheddar cheese (garnish)
sour cream (garnish)

Trim the beef and cut it into 1-inch cubes. Heat the oil in a stovetop Dutch oven or other suitable pot. Brown the beef, working in three batches. Remove each batch with a slotted spoon and set aside. Cook the onion and garlic for 5 minutes, stirring as you go with a wooden spoon. Add the chili powder, cumin, salt, and Tabasco, stirring for another minute. Drain the canned chiles and add to the pot, along with the water. Bring to a boil, add the beef, reduce the heat to very low, cover tightly, and simmer for 1½ hours, or until the beef is tender. (With tough beef you may have to add a little more water and cook quite a bit longer.) Serve over rice. Top with chopped onion, shredded cheese, and sour cream, if wanted. Feeds 4 to 6.

Note: If the onion, cheese, and sour cream are not served, it's really best to put the hot chili into a large bowl, then add a dollop of rice in the middle instead of serving the red over the white.

15

CHILI WITH SECRETS

Sometimes the secret of one's chili depends on an unexpected and outrageous ingredient. As often as not, the ingredient isn't held secret at all and in fact depends on revelation, and, in some cases, the ingredient really doesn't make all that much difference, except possibly in the mind of the cook and partaker. Often something as common as beer is touted as the secret ingredient, and I have seen single recipes with as many as three "secret" ingredients, all revealed in the ingredients list.

Sometimes the "secret" of a good chili doesn't entail an ingredient. It can also mean the "key" to making the chili. Often such secrets lie in the cooking techniques, not in the list of ingredients. In my experience, a major secret of this sort is long, slow simmering.

Chapter 6 contains a wealth of information and suggestions for secret ingredients, and other secrets are revealed in recipes through-out the book. Here are a few more to consider:

Chili with Bitters

Among the ingredients for this rather lengthy recipe, adapted here from Sunset magazine's book All-Time Favorite Recipes, I was surprised to find that the list calls for 3 tablespoons of aromatic bitters. I knew, of course, that bitters are often used in mixed drinks and sometimes in foods—but in chili? Well, why not? All chiliheads should know that bitters are sometimes used as a digestif and as a cure for hangovers.

2 pounds lean ground beef
2 (15-ounce) cans red kidney beans, drained and washed
1 large (28-ounce) can tomatoes
1 can (15-ounce) tomato puree
1 can beer
1 large onion, chopped
3 cloves garlic, minced
3 tablespoons Worcestershire sauce
3 tablespoons aromatic bitters
2 dried bay leaves
1 tablespoon chili powder
1 teaspoon crushed red pepper flakes
1 teaspoon ground cumin
1 teaspoon ground coriander seeds
1 teaspoon dry thyme
1 teaspoon dry oregano
1 teaspoon dry basil
1 beef bouillon cube
shredded cheddar cheese (garnish)
sour cream (garnish)
sliced green onions (garnish)

Brown the beef in a stovetop Dutch oven or other suitable pot. Add the chopped onion and cook for 5 minutes, stirring as you go with a wooden spoon. Chop the tomatoes and add them to the pot, along with the liquid from the can, tomato puree, beans, Worcestershire, bitters, beer, garlic, bouillon cube, chili powder, red pepper flakes, bay leaves, coriander, cumin, thyme, oregano, and basil. Bring all this to a boil, reduce the heat to very low, and simmer—do not boil—uncovered for about 2 hours, or until the meat is very tender and the chili is thick. (Be sure to stir a few times toward the end, adding a little water if needed.) Serve hot in bowls, with the cheddar, sour cream, and sliced green onions on the side.

Note: This recipe contains very little chile. Increase the measure of the chili powder if you like, or add a hefty dose of pure chile powder if you want to deepen the red color and texture.

Wild Onion Chili

I make this recipe with a wild onion that grows profusely in my yard. Any wild onion or garlic, or ramp, will do, but remember that some of these are quite strong. Substitute fresh garden garlic if you must.

- 4 pounds ground round beef or venison
- 1 pound bulk sausage
- 3–4 cups chicken stock
- ⅓ cup ancho chile powder
- ¼ cup minced wild onions with part of green tops
- 1 tablespoon whole cumin seeds
- 2 teaspoons freshly ground black pepper
- 2 teaspoons sea salt (or to taste)

Lightly toast the cumin seeds in a small skillet for a couple of minutes (shaking the skillet a time or two to prevent the seeds from scorching) and grind with mortar and pestle. If you plan to cook the chili for a long time, grinding the cumin seeds isn't necessary. Brown the sausage in a cast-iron Dutch oven or other suitable pot. Brown the beef a pound or so at a time, stirring it into the rest. Pour off the oil that has accumulated, or ladle it off, unless you want your chili greasy-spoon style. Stir in the wild onion. Add 3 cups of the chicken stock. Bring to a boil and stir in the ancho powder a little at a time. Stir in the cumin powder, black pepper, and salt. Reduce the heat to very low and simmer the chili for 2 hours or longer, adding a little more chicken stock or water if needed. Stir and taste frequently. Serve hot in bowls or spoon over rice or pasta.

For this secret recipe, beans and other go-withs (except for rice or pasta) should be served strictly on the side. The chili, in short, should be almost pure meat. That is the real secret to this recipe, not the few wild onions or chicken stock listed.

A. D.'s Gourmet Cuitlacoche Chili

I offer this recipe with fear and trembling, lest I be accused of adding outrageous stuff to a bowl of red. Some of the Texas good ol' boys might have had enough by now and consider this modest contribution to be the last straw. If they should run me down and threaten to string me up, however, I want to point out in my defense that I have at least kept the ingredients list fairly short.

The secret ingredient here is, of course, cuitlacoche, *which turns the bowl of red a dark mahogany hue and gives it a deep, earthy flavor unlike any other. If your guests want to know the secret, don't tell them right off, waiting perhaps well into the second bowl. If they press for an answer, tell them the secret ingredient is cuitlacoche, as the Mexicans and modern-day gourmets call it. If they press for more detail, tell them it's sometimes called corn truffle. It's best to draw the line here, unless you think they can handle the plain truth, in which case go ahead and tell them it's corn smut— that awful-looking black fungus that sometimes grows like a cancer on an innocent ear of green corn.*

I once told my father, a farmer, that the smut on a roasting ear in question was edible. He said, shoot, he wouldn't eat that stuff for a million dollars. Most other farmers will no doubt feel the same way, although in today's market the smut is worth far more than the corn, if you can find a buyer in your neck of the woods. Cuitlacoche is sometimes available fresh in gourmet markets, and I have heard that it is actually cultivated these days. Personally, I either find my own in a cornfield or garden or buy canned cuitlacoche from Mexico.

> 5 pounds tough beef, diced
> ½ pound finely diced hog jowls
> 1 (16-ounce) can cuitlacoche
> 2 large onions, chopped
> scant ½ cup ancho chili powder
> red pepper flakes to taste (wild bird peppers if available)
> 1 tablespoon cumin seeds (or to taste)
> salt and black pepper to taste
> water as needed

Try out the hog jowls in a cast-iron stovetop Dutch oven. Brown the onion in the pan drippings. Lightly brown the beef a little at a time. Slowly sprinkle on the chili powder, stirring as you go. Add the salt and red pepper flakes. Hold the black pepper. Add enough water to barely cover the meat. Open the can of cuitlacoche with your head turned (if you look at it, you might well chicken out), dump it into the pot, and stir it into the chili. Add the cumin seeds. Bring to a boil, reduce the heat to very low, cover tightly, and simmer for 4 or 5 hours. Stir from time to time, adding more water as needed, to prevent burning on the bottom. Serve hot in bowls with soft corn tortillas and bowls of chilled salsa and luscious guacamole on the side. Season to taste with black pepper.

This is a wonderful chili if you like the earthy flavors of corn and aren't put off by the appearance of the smut.

Randy Moore's Four-Dump Secret

Pendery's, the chile and spice company in Dallas, markets a chili mix said to be used in Randy Moore's winning recipe for the Terlingua 2001. The recipe starts on the main package and continues on the four dump pouches.

  2 pounds cubed chuck tender beef
  1 (14½-ounce) can Swanson's Beef Broth
  1 (8-ounce) can Swanson's Contadina Tomato Sauce
  1 kit Randy Moore's 4-Dump Chili Mix
  1 jalapeño
  1 serrano
  salt and cayenne to taste

Brown the beef lightly in a stovetop Dutch oven, stirring as you go. Add the beef broth, tomato sauce, and dump #1. Float the jalapeño and the serrano. Bring to a boil and add dump #2. Reduce the heat and simmer for an hour. Add dump #3. Stir in and simmer for approximately 30 minutes. Squeeze the jalapeño and serrano, discarding the pulp. Stir in dump #4, salt, and cayenne to taste. Serve hot.

Author's comment: Clearly the secret of this chili lies in the contents of the dumps, the ingredients of which are required by law to be printed on the package in the order of greatest quantity. Dump #1 (a total of 0.8 ounce) contained the following: hydrolyzed vegetable protein, salt, dextrose, beef fat, caramel color, citric acid, spice extractives, disodium inosinate, guanylate, silica, maltodextrin, modified food starch, sugar, onion, yeast extract, oleoresin, turmeric, natural and artificial flavoring, and other spices. Dump #2 (0.08 pound): garlic, onion, coriander, cumin, salt, black pepper, red peppers, monosodium glutamate, yellow 5 tricalcium phosphate, annatto, natural spices, and less than 2 percent silica. Dump #3 (0.06 pound): salt, cumin, oregano, onion, garlic, black pepper, cayenne, coriander, annatto, yellow 5 tricalcium phosphate, red pepper, monosodium glutamate, natural spices, and less than 2 percent silica. Dump #4 (0.02 pound): cumin, cayenne, yellow tricalcium phosphate, coriander, annatto, salt, and natural spices.

At the end of the ingredients list on packet #4, the text says, "Now you know the secrets of a CASI winner!" Yeah. Sure we do.

In closing out this short chapter, I might add that many of the ingredients listed in modern chili recipes *ought* to be kept secret. Personally, if I felt the need to put prunes into my chili, I sure as hell wouldn't tell anybody. On the other hand, champions of the prune might well feel the same way about cuitlacoche.

16

REGIONAL AND INSTITUTIONAL CHILI

Regional differences in chili are not as sharply defined as we have been led to believe, and the big question—to bean or not to bean?—is not always argued over geographical lines, once you leave Texas. There are a few regional trends, however, and these are discussed under the headings below, along with some institutional varieties such as Committee Cookbook Chili, Family Cookbook Chili, and Cook-Off Chili.

MEXICAN CHILI

Some modern writers on Mexican cuisine are a little on the snooty side and disclaim any ethnic connection to chile con carne, dismissing it as Tex-Mex junk food. One modern chili book author even said the only thing that food scholars agree on is that chile con carne originated in the United States, not in Mexico. Well, this is nonsense to me, although I don't claim to be a scholar, chili or otherwise. Because the chile pepper came into the United States from Mexico, it's only logical that chile con carne was first made there. In fact, Elisabeth Lambert Ortiz, in the first edition of her excellent *The Complete Book of Mexican Cooking*, set forth a recipe said to be the authentic northern Mexican style of cooking chili. It contains beef cut into ½-inch cubes along with lard, ancho peppers, onion, garlic, oregano, salt, freshly ground pepper, and kidney beans. The beans are cooked separately, she says, and added to the chili pot during the last few minutes of the cooking. Apart from the beans, the main difference between this dish and Texas chili is that this one doesn't have cumin. Thus, the recipe is similar to the early chilis we cooked in chapter 1. Ms. Ortiz adds that cumin may be used instead of, or in addition to, the oregano. (In the first edition of this work, no distinction was made between regular oregano and Mexican oregano.) She says that the addition of tomatoes is frowned upon by purists, including herself.

See also George C. Booth's Mexican Chili recipe in chapter 14. Booth allows beans, cumin, tomatoes, and cornmeal.

Note also that the Mexicans cook up lots of meat stews, cooked very slowly in a mole, a sauce made from chili peppers, onion, and other ingredients, including chocolate, an old Aztec favorite (which helps explain why this odd ingredient pops up in a number of chili recipes north of the border). Many of these mole dishes are very, very close to chile con carne. But, hey, if the Mexicans choose to disclaim chili as one of their national culinary treasures, I say we ought to take it, along with Texas.

Texas Chili

Although chili is now the official food of the Lone Star State, there is no defining recipe. Tomato and tomato products are allowed in some recipes, but not in others. Usually beans can be eaten with the chili as long as they are not cooked in the same pot. Not even pinto beans, sometimes called Texas caviar, should be cooked in the same pot, purists say. Personally, I think that Texans got so tired of pinto beans back during the cowboy days that they want at least one important dish without them. As the story goes, a cowboy went into a restaurant at the end of a cattle drive to Dodge City and ordered everything on the menu that did not contain beans.

All joking aside, the defining ingredient in early Texas chili was prepared chili powder and mixes, including a dose of cumin. Indeed, Texas is where chili powder got its start commercially, being the home of both Gephardt's and Pendery's. A few real Texas chiliheads, however—usually a culinary cut above the beer-drinking good ol' boys—are returning to the pure chile pepper powder, used directly in the chili or for making their own powder blend. Of course, these people tend to go overboard in their search for the right stuff. A recipe published in a Texas cookbook, for example, lists, in addition to both ground cumin and whole cumin seeds, the following pepper measures: 1 tablespoon ground chilies passillas, 1 teaspoon crushed chilies quebrados (piquins), 5 jalapeños, 5 chiles anchos, 1 dried chile New Mexico (big red one), and 2 dried Jap chiles (little skinny red ones). The recipe also calls for a 1-ounce square of unsweetened chocolate.

A lot of Texans insist that small chunks of beef should be used instead of ground beef, or that a special "chili grind" meat be used. The chili grind is quite coarse as compared with regular ground meat. All this sounds good, but the truth is that most family chili in Texas is made these days with ordinary supermarket ground meat. A good many of the recipes also call for beer, usually Tecate or some other Mexican brand.

Generally speaking, the character of the Texans is just as important as the recipe. As Linda West Eckhardt said of Texans in her *Only Texas Cookbook,* "They love to serve chili to outlanders and watch their eyes water. They love to argue about the ingredients and origin of the state dish of Texas. As a result, recipes for the fiery dish have proliferated faster than a family of rabbits."

Examples of typical Texas chili recipes can be found here and there in this book. One of the best is Chili According to Mel Marshall in chapter 14.

CALIFORNIA CHILI

At the cook-off level, early California chili was influenced by a reaction to Texas chili as represented in the Terlingua cook-offs. This event split into two factions, and one of these pulled out and moved to California. From the outset these California chiliheads were rather freewheeling and more liberal than the Texas good ol' boys. All manner of ingredients were allowed in chili, partly to rile the Texans.

These days, we are likely to see most anything in California chili, including various wines and prunes.

NEW MEXICAN CHILI

The chile pepper, both green and dried, is very important to the agricultural economy of New Mexico. This, in turn, has an influence on the state's chili. Green chili stew is an important regional dish, and is becoming more popular outside the area as fresh peppers become more widely available. This trend is expected to continue. Red chili is more likely to be made from scratch in New Mexico than in any other state, whereas in Texas the dried chile powder is more prevalent. There are some firm opinions in New Mexico on whether ground or cubed beef should be used, as well as about proper and improper ingredients such as beans—but these matters are not hotly contested in New Mexico, for the most part.

See the green chili recipes in chapter 7, and be sure to try the two recipes below.

New Mexican Red

Here's an adaption of a recipe from Corona, New Mexico, as reported in The National Cowboy Hall of Fame Chuck Wagon Cookbook. *The chile peppers range from mild to medium hot.*

Sauce Caribe

15 dried New Mexican chile peppers
2 (16-ounce) cans tomatoes
4 cups boiling water
4 cloves garlic
1 teaspoon freshly ground cumin (or more to taste)
1 teaspoon dried oregano

Remove the stems, seeds, and inner veins of the chile peppers. Reserve some of the seeds. Soak the peppers in the boiling water for 2 minutes, or until they are soft. Drain the seeds and put ¼ cup of the soaking liquid into a blender, along with the chiles, tomatoes, garlic, cumin, and oregano. Blend until you have a smooth sauce. Taste. If you want it hotter, add some of the chile seeds. Cover and refrigerate until needed. Also save what's left of the soaking liquid.

The Chili

5 pounds beef chuck, cut into ½-inch cubes
1 recipe Sauce Caribe (above) and soaking liquid
¼ cup vegetable oil (maybe more)
4 medium onions, chopped
¼ cup yellow cornmeal
2 teaspoons salt or to taste
hot water

Using about half the oil in a stovetop Dutch oven, brown the beef in batches and drain. Add the rest of the oil and cook the onions for about 5 minutes, stirring from time to time as you go. Add the beef back to the pot along with the recipe of Sauce Caribe and the chile soaking liquid. Stir in the salt and bring to a boil. Reduce the heat to very low, cover, and simmer for about 2 hours, stirring and adding a little water if needed to keep the chili on the thin side. In a small bowl, mix the cornmeal with ½ cup hot water. Pour a little at a time into the chili pot, stirring well, and cook for about 5 minutes. Use as much of the cornmeal as needed to make the chili as thick as you want it.

Pueblo Red Chile

Here's an unusual recipe from the modern-day Pueblo of the Southwest, said to be served on Feast Day. There are, of course, a number of variations on the recipe, and this one has been adapted from Foods of the Southwest Indian Nations: Native American Recipes, *a collection by Lois Ellen Frank. Note that it contains a goodly amount of chile powder—but no cumin. It also contains an unusual ingredient for chili: diced potatoes.*

1 pound ground beef chuck
8 medium russet potatoes, peeled and cubed
1 large onion, diced
¼ cup New Mexico or Anaheim red chile powder
1 tablespoon olive oil
1 teaspoon salt
¼ teaspoon dried oregano
hot water

Heat the oil in a cast-iron skillet and brown the beef. Reduce the heat and sauté the onion for 3 or 4 minutes, stirring in the chile powder with a wooden spoon as you go. Set aside. In a saucepan, bring about 6 cups of hot water to a boil. Add the meat-and-onion mixture. Bring to a new boil, reduce the heat to very low, cover tightly, and simmer for 2 hours. Add about 2 more cups of boiling water, potatoes, oregano, and salt. Simmer for 15 minutes, or until the potatoes are soft. If the consistency of the stew isn't as you like it, either add more water to thin it or boil it longer to reduce it.

MIDWESTERN CHILI

The use of pasta distinguishes midwestern chili from the rest. Elbow macaroni and spaghetti are the most common forms, but, of course, these days we see most any kind, al dente or not. Lots of tomato products and spices are used in many of the recipes, and allspice is always used. Beans are allowed in midwestern chili, with the only argument being whether they are cooked in the pot or separately.

Cincinnati, Ohio, claims to be the chili capital of the world, and some people believe the dish originated there. The exact recipe, however, is open to question. The notion of serving pasta with chili reportedly originated in two local food chains, The Empress and the Skyline. Although some pasta is sometimes cooked in the chili and left in the pot, it's more often than not used as a bed for the chili, all served up on a plate. Many restaurants in the Midwest (and elsewhere) offer it two-way, three-way, four-way, and five-way, depending on what is used to top a bed of spaghetti (or other pasta) and a layer of chili.

Believe it or not, serving pasta with chili is now quite widespread in the United States. It's not uncommon even in Texas, where it is sometimes called spaghetti red.

In Illinois chili is sometimes spelled "chilli" with two l's, especially in the Springfield area. This dates back to a sign painted on the window of a local chili parlor some years ago. Of course, this inspires the Texans to say that midwesterners don't even know how to spell chili, much less how to make it properly.

Personally, I approve of the basic menu of serving chili with pasta but I really prefer to have more chile pepper in the pot, either as powder or pulp from dried red chiles, than most of the midwestern recipes call for. The latest edition of *The Joy of Cooking,* for example, set forth a recipe called Cincinnati Chili Cockaigne, following a short discussion of the chili offered by The Empress, one of the two early chili parlors. The recipe calls for ground chuck (2 pounds), onions, garlic, tomato sauce (15 ounces), cider vinegar, a quart of water, and Worcestershire, along with the following spices: peppercorns, allspice, cloves, bay leaf, salt, cinnamon, cayenne (1½ teaspoons), cumin (1 teaspoon), and unsweetened chocolate. Well, this might make a pretty good spaghetti sauce, but for chili I insist on more chile pulp. Lots more. And H. Allen Smith would no doubt ask for more cumin.

Some recipes for Cincinnati chili call for even more spices. One in Bill Bridges' *The Great Chili Book,* for example, calls for chile powder (or chile molido), paprika, black pepper, cumin, marjoram, allspice, cinnamon, cloves, mace, coriander, cardamom, bay leaf, and salt to taste. The instructions ask us to sprinkle the salt over the bottom of a hot skillet before browning the meat and onions. The author adds that to get the chili right the cook should "add spices one at a time, tasting after each addition. When the taste is right, stop adding ingredients. If the first attempt misses, the next time start adding spices from the other end of the list. Up to a teaspoon of turmeric may do it. Start off with ¼ to ½ teaspoon and work up."

In any case, the practice of serving leftover chili with pasta makes sense. I normally cook a big batch of chili (without beans) and freeze the leftovers in 1-cup containers, just right for topping individual servings of spaghetti, followed by a generous sprinkling of grated cheese. Good stuff, served with rolled warm tortillas or even with a chewy French or Italian bread.

YANKEE CHILI

People in the Northeast tend to put lots of beans into chili, possibly because of the tradition of Boston baked beans in the area. Personally, I am a great fan of Boston baked beans if they are made right—that is, with plenty of salt pork and molasses or real (unrefined) brown sugar—but their flavor is really lost to the cumin in chili. In this matter I tend to agree with Elisabeth Lambert Ortiz, author of *The Complete Book of Mexican Cooking:* Beans for chile con carne are plainly cooked, although I do doctor up my pinto beans somewhat. In any case, beans are popular in Yankee chili, and some recipes call for several kinds. One Maine recipe calls for yellow eye beans, whatever these are.

Perhaps this area's most significant contribution is the use of chili on hot dogs. Many call this chili Coney Sauce because the hot dog is connected historically to Coney Island.

SUPERMARKET CHILI

Every American supermarket carries chili powder in the spice section and a chili mix in the canned or packaged gravy section, and sometimes scattered around the store, perhaps at the ground beef counter, as impulse items. All of these have recipes printed on the package. Most of the instructions are quite simple, and tend

161

to offer the cook several options, such as ground beef or ground turkey. The idea here is to please everybody and offend no one. These recipes are also easy to prepare and quick to cook, and make for an inexpensive and nutritious meal. For all these reasons supermarket chili is a practical choice for the family cook, many of whom, these days, are looking for a quick supper after a hard day at the workplace.

Canned chili is also available in supermarkets, and it is one of the most widely used canned meat products. Some of it isn't bad, either, and various brands are available with and without beans. Read the can label. As with the quick recipes discussed above, canned chili can usually be improved by adding a little stuff to it, such as sautéed onion and seasonings. Sauté the onion in bacon drippings or a little cooking oil, then add the contents of the can and reheat.

Here is a sample supermarket recipe:

McCormick's 20 Minute Chili

This large spice outfit offers several kinds of chili powder and mixes, with little difference between the spice rack powder (marketed in a box or jar) and the gravy section mix (marketed in a sealed plastic pouch). This recipe is from the latter kind.

    1 pound ground beef or ground turkey
    2 (8-ounce) cans tomato sauce or 1 (14½-ounce) can tomatoes,
        broken up
    1 (15-ounce) can kidney beans, undrained
    1 (1.25-ounce) pouch McCormick's Original Chili Seasoning

Brown the meat in a skillet and drain off the fat. Stir in the chili seasoning, tomato sauce or tomatoes, and kidney beans. Bring to a boil, cover, and simmer for 10 minutes. Serve hot in bowls. Makes 4 servings, McCormick says.

This is an acceptable chili, but many cooks, usually men, will want to improve on it, or at least add to it. If you are so inclined, start with a little chopped onion browned in bacon drippings, and end with a little salt and black pepper to taste.

Committee Cookbook Chili

Every hick town and crossroads in the county has at least one committee cookbook made up of recipes from contributors. These are usually published to raise money for some civic or church organization, which usually foots the printing bill and sells copies locally. Although most of the committee cookbooks tend to be regional, some are published by associations with members from around the country. Also, some local books contain recipes from various parts of the country or world. A retirement community in Florida, for example, might have lots of recipes from points north.

In any case, almost all of these books contain a quick-cook chili made from canned and packaged supermarket ingredients. The ingredients lists always comprise plastic-wrapped ground beef, chili powder, canned tomato products, and at least one kind of canned bean. Minor variations in volume and supplemental ingredients are infinite, however, so that one contributor's recipe is a little different from another's. Those recipes contributed by men tend to have more added ingredients and sport colorful names, such as Ben's Hellfire and Damnation Chili, Dr. Toon's Buzzard Breath Chili, or Ed's Tailwind Chili, although all such recipes might be quite benign, as chili goes.

These cookbook recipes are very close to the supermarket chili set forth above, but with a difference. Because the cook's name will be associated with the recipe, most people will add at least a pinch or two of at least half a dozen spices, along with a hefty dose of garlic powder. Women usually keep the length of the ingredients list rather short, but some men might end up with a recipe calling for three or more ingredients. Good ol' boys should know that such recipes can often be improved on by the use of freshly chopped garlic and onions instead of spice rack powdered products, and almost all of them can stand a hefty addition of pure chile powder or chile paste.

Fund-Raiser Cookbook Chili

Here's a recipe from a committee-type cookbook (Stove Pilot, put together by air force wives at Maxwell Air Force Base in Alabama) that makes use of lots of canned stuff. It's quick, tasty, and filling, and will do quite nicely if you're in a hurry to feed the kids.

- 1 pound ground beef (chuck)
- 2 (16-ounce) cans tomatoes
- 2 (16-ounce) cans red kidney beans
- 2 tablespoons Crisco
- 2 tablespoons Gephardt's chili powder
- 1 large onion, finely chopped
- 1 clove garlic, minced

In a stovetop Dutch oven or large skillet, sauté the onions and garlic for 5 or 6 minutes in Crisco, stirring as you go. Add and brown the ground meat and sprinkle on the chili powder. Stir in the tomatoes and kidney beans. Bring to a boil, reduce the heat, cover, and simmer for about 20 minutes. Serve hot in bowls.

FAMILY COOKBOOK CHILI

The development of chili in America, as well as the growing popularity of chile peppers in our national cuisine, is reflected in the many editions of *The Joy of Cooking*. The first edition, published in 1931—during the middle of the Great Depression—did not offer a recipe for chili, although it was and is a perfect hard-times food. The only chili listing in the index (which, oddly, is set forth in the front of the book) is for a chili sauce, which is similar to modern salsa or chowchow, made with lots of green pepper and other ingredients.

Nor is there a listing in the index for any of the Mexican, southwestern, Cajun, California, or other peppers. Not even bell pepper is listed. What *is* listed, however, are recipes for Pepper Casings—or stuffed bell peppers! One of these, called Pepper Cases with Creamed Oysters, looks tempting, but unfortunately it's beyond the scope of this book.

By 1964 *The Joy of Cooking* had become larger and fatter, now with 849 pages and with the index moved to the back of the book. It contained only a single recipe for chili con carne, calling for both beans and tomatoes as well as chopped onions. A short text on pepper treated them for the most part as a spice, right along with black pepper. These include brief mentions of ancho, but most of the emphasis was on paprika, cayenne, and Tabasco.

A recipe for chili powder called for 3 tablespoons paprika, ⅛ teaspoon cayenne, and 1 tablespoon turmeric, along with "plenty of" garlic. Note that if this powder is used in the chili recipe (as is recommended), you would have a chili without much chile pulp and no cumin. A note, however, explained that cumin, oregano, coriander, and clove, along with "sweet and hot" peppers, could also be used.

Chili and chile peppers had come of age in my copy of the 1997 edition of *Joy,* grown now to 1,136 pages. It contains five recipes for chili, one of which starts us off by making our own chili powder. Recommended go-withs include rice and sour cream. A variation on this recipe allows black or pinto beans. A recipe for camp chili calls for the usual stuff, along with a 1-pound can of kidney beans with juice, a 1-pound can of great northern beans with juice, and a 1-pound can of pinto beans with juice. (One can only hope that we are not camping in a closed tent!) Another recipe is for a Cincinnati chili, as discussed above under "Midwestern Chili." Finally, we have an interesting recipe called Ohio Farmhouse Sausage Chili, containing pork sausage, celery, canned tomatoes, beans, and so on. The spices include sage, which goes nicely with most pork sausage. The chili is served with cubed sharp cheddar cheese, buttermilk biscuits, or "Northern" corn bread.

This edition of *Joy* also contains an excellent and very helpful discussion—seven jam-packed pages—of the various kinds of chile peppers, red and green, with instructions on how to handle them. There is even a good recipe for New Mexican chili powder. Although there are a lot of problems in this big book, at least to me, the coverage on chili and chile peppers is a step in the right direction. Chili and chiles have come of age in American cookery. There's joy in that.

Cook-Off Chili

The great chili cook-offs started by H. Allen Smith, Wick Fowler, and others in Texas during the 1960s and '70s greatly increased the interest in chili, owing mostly to the publicity and the crowing. These started with a cook-off in Terlingua, a ghost town in the Big Bend area of Texas. Later the members split, forming two separate organizations. Anyone interested in competitive chili cook-offs should get in touch with both outfits.

International Chili Society (ICS), PO Box 1027, San Juan Capistrano, CA 92693. Phone: (877) 777-4427. Website: www.chili cookoff.com. This is the largest organization and started as a California spin-off from the first cook-offs down in Terlingua. *Chile Pepper Magazine* is affiliated with ICS and is sent to members. Note that at least some of the ICS cook-offs have a separate category for green chili.

Chili Appreciation Society International (CASI), 2 Green Cedar Road, Boerne, TX 85730. Website: www.chili.org. This organization grew from the original Terlingua cook-offs and is still greatly influenced by Texans. The annual championship cook-off is held each year in Terlingua, but about 500 regional contests lead up to the main event. If you want to get in touch, try the website. It will give you the rules of the game and put you in touch with *Terlingua Trails,* a newsletter that keeps members informed of upcoming cook-offs around the country. *The Goat Gap Gazette* also covers the competition.

For the most part, chili cook-offs are great fun for the contestants and should not be taken too seriously by anybody. I don't compete in these events, but I like to practice my lifelong role of a very helpful, much amused, deeply knowledgeable, well-meaning, and sometimes maligned kibitzer. I truly do applaud such events, usually staged for a charitable cause, but the professional chef and the advanced amateurs, whether they win or lose, should not take the verdict of the judges as much more than the result of random selection. This is especially true of the smaller local cook-offs.

If you enter such an event and lose, chalk it up to mere mathematics based on how those incompetent judges cast their votes. Some judges like their chili hot, some like it sweet. If you want to increase your chances of winning, find the statistical norm, cook a reasonable chili according to the rules of the cook-off, add a little more cumin to your recipes, and, for show and presentation, get a tall white chef's hat and apron with red chile peppers on them. You'll win some cook-offs if you play the game and stick with it long enough. When you do win, you can thank your lucky stars that you have finally found a group of judges with good sense, impeccable taste, and uncommon fairness.

I have perused a number of recipes for winning chili, but, frankly, I couldn't make heads or tails of why they won. It could be that the recipes, as they end up in a book or article, or on the Internet, do not necessarily reflect what's actually in the chili that the judges taste. After several hours of cooking and drinking beer, tasting and adjusting the contents of the pot as they go, some of the contestants don't really know what's in the chili, or at least don't know the exact measures. Often another small box of cayenne stirred into a huge pot of chili won't make much difference.

The ingredients to be used in cook-off chili are regulated somewhat by rules. One of the major chili societies requires that the contestants must at least taste their own chili—and prohibits the discharge of firearms on the premises!

While writing this book, I visited the annual chili competition on St. George Island, Florida, held the first weekend in March under the auspices of the International Chili Society. Most of the contestants, some with tall chile pepper hats and colorful chef's aprons, were busy chopping onions, mincing garlic, dicing beef, and so on. Some of these were free to talk but reluctant to give up any secrets; others, often with a beer in hand, had loose tongues. Of course, I didn't believe a word they said. No matter. Talk really wasn't necessary. I could tell by their lack of adeptness with the chef's knife that they were for the most part jacklegs, which is as it should be.

Among the ingredients on the preparation tables, I noted a surprisingly widespread use of canned chicken stock and beef stock, along with the usual tomato products. A few of the cooks were using a pure chile powder and cumin, but most went with a simple chili spice mix. Pots? Mostly tall stainless steel with a few cast-iron pieces. Almost all of them cooked on a propane-fired three-legged turkey-fryer rig, but a few used little gas stoves that sat on a table.

On the whole, I found the cook-off and the contestants to be great fun, but I'll have to admit that I sampled the chili with uncharacteristic restraint, partly because I had consumed two dozen Apalachicola oysters on the half shell shortly before crossing the long bridge that led out to the island. I had never before mixed raw oysters and chili, and I was naturally a little concerned about the gastric chemistry even before I came to a conspicuous open-tent pavilion, well tasseled, in the far corner of the arena. Out front in plain view of the passersby was a shiny new coffin atop a long, narrow table with the following placard under a funeral wreath:

Here lies Willie
Who ate our Chili.

PART FOUR

Using and Serving Chili

Chapter 17 is about using chili to top hot dogs, fill tacos, and so on. Often leftover chili can be used for these purposes. In most cases, the chili is cooked separately and used as an ingredient, but in a few recipes, such as making meat loaf, the chili ingredients can be incorporated in the main recipe.

Chili is traditionally served in a bowl with crackers or tortillas on the side. These days we find that chili is being topped or flanked with a wide variety of foods and garnish. Some of the more appropriate go-withs, such as refried beans, tortillas, and sour cream, are covered in chapter 18.

17

CHILI DOGS, WRAPS, AND LOAVES

Ella Mae Dory spoke of a Halloween bonfire for a gathering of parents and children in the book *Ella Mae's Cajun Kitchen,* featuring the cooking at Avery Island in Louisiana, where the world-famous Tabasco Sauce is bottled. Hot dogs were the main event, roasted, she said, on bamboo sticks, then put into warm buns and topped with a scoop of chili. The recipe for the chili was set forth, revealing it for the first time in 50 years, she said. It is made with ground beef, chopped yellow onions, chopped celery, chopped bell peppers, and tomato paste, along with a little chili powder and, of course, some Tabasco Sauce. The secret to the chili, she says, is in long, slow simmering—and in adding part of the chili powder to some flour and stirring in some water to make a paste, which is added near the end of the cooking time. Well, it's a good chili albeit without much chile pulp, but I don't see anything that sets it off as a *hot dog* chili. In any case, Ella Mae gives us another use of the chili. The partakers, she says, sometimes have small bags of Fritos. These they open—and put a scoop of chili right into the bag! What a mess.

Some people call hot dog chili Coney Sauce or Coney Chili. Again, looking at recipes from around the country, it's hard to see what sets these recipes apart from regular chili. I have included one of the recipes in this chapter, along with my own take on a hot dog sauce. The only thing I can say for certain about Coney Sauce is that it should be made with finely ground meat as compared to the regular chili grind. If you use market-grind meat, I suggest that you brown it lightly in a skillet, stirring to break up all the chunks. Then zap for a few seconds in a food processor or food mill before proceeding with the recipe.

Any good chili can be used as a topping, but I think the beanless kind works best. Most of the canned hot dog chili sauces in supermarkets are not up to snuff. One that I tested doesn't even have meat in it. Instead, it has "cracked beans," which, I suppose, makes the texture a little like chili with ground meat. If you want to use a canned sauce, I suggest that you purchase a good canned chili without beans. Use it as a sauce, perhaps adding a few finely diced sautéed onions or something to make it your own.

The box for a commercial chili mix known as Hard Times Chili (as discussed in chapter 4) recommends an interesting variation on the Coney Dog. Put a steamed or boiled dog into a bun and place it on a small serving platter. Spoon a generous serving of chili over the bun, letting it spill over into the plate. Cover with shredded cheese and chopped onions. Eat with a knife and fork!

The recipes in this chapter also cover some other ways of using chili. These are especially recommended for using up leftovers. Here are a few other serving suggestions, gleaned partly, but not entirely, from Bill Bridges' *The Great Chili Book*.

1. A Hot Soak is a cone, similar to those used to hold a scoop of ice cream, made out of saltine crackers. A good scoop of chili (about 4 ounces) fills the cone.

2. A Chili-Mac is a bed of pasta, often macaroni, topped with chili. Sometimes called Midwest chili or Cincinnati chili, discussed in chapter 16.

3. A Mac à la Mode is a Chili-Mac topped with two fried eggs, a dish from Hodges restaurant in St. Louis.

4. A Slinger is another creation from Hodges. It's served on a platter, with two cheese-topped hamburger patties with a fried egg on one side and fried potatoes on the other, all covered with chili.

5. A Super Slinger is a regular Slinger topped with a tamale.

6. A Chili Burger is a meat patty topped with chili. This can be served open faced on a bun or sandwiched.

7. Wet Shoes are french fries topped with chili.

While I don't endorse the practice, I have read about one chili being used as a go-with or side dish to grilled steak.

In any case, here are a few recipes to try.

Ed's Chili Dog

In my small hometown a fellow named Ed Posey ran a combined raw bar and hot dog joint. He claimed to have the world's best hot dog and advertised accordingly with signs on the roads leading into town. The dogs were very good all right, and I published an article about them in an airline in-flight magazine. Ed wouldn't give out the recipe for his chili topping, and has since passed on. I guess he took the secret to the grave with him. I think it was a mixture of finely ground pork and beef, seasoned mostly with salt and black pepper. It wasn't red, and I don't think it contained chile peppers, except maybe for a little hot sauce. It definitely contained no beans. In short, it was simply a meat sauce seasoned with salt and black pepper. The "chili" was so good that many people ordered a chili dog—without the wiener. Ed considered the chili topping to be standard, but he offered the hot dogs with or without chopped onions. Catsup was available at the counter.

I have made a similar chili for hot dogs, using some ancho powder—but no cumin. In fact, I must have made a dozen or more variations, one of which I published in another book, but I finally gave up trying to match Ed's sauce and looked to my own recipe complete with chile powder. This mix can be used to make a chili dog, or as a topping for a regular hot dog. It's important to remember, however, that the techniques of making the chili and putting the dog together are as important as the sauce recipe.

I once mentioned "Coney Sauce" to Ed. He looked at me with a blank expression on his face, as if he expected me to tell him more. After 50 years of making hot dogs, the guy didn't even know the term! He wasn't blank about putting sauerkraut on hot dogs, however; instead he was a little shocked by the notion and he suspected that I was pulling his leg.

When making the following recipe, it's best to use a fatty ground beef and pork. If you use lean meat, add some bacon drippings or melted suet.

1 pound market-grind beef hamburger
1 pound ground pork
¼ cup ancho powder
1 cup beef stock
1 cup water (more if needed)
salt and black pepper to taste

Brown the ground beef and pork in a skillet. Sprinkle on the ancho powder and cook for a few more minutes, stirring as you go, until the pieces of meat are all separated. Put the mixture into a food processor and pulse it a time or two, until the meats are finely ground. Put the mess back into the skillet or a pot. Add the beef stock and water, along with salt and freshly ground black pepper. Simmer for an hour or longer. Leave the chili simmering in the pot until needed.

When you are ready to make the hot dogs, steam the buns lightly, until soft but not mushy. Boil or steam the wieners (or grill them) until hot. Put a wiener into a bun and top with a ladle of chili sauce, well drained. That is, you ladle a portion of the chili out of the pot with a strainer, then let the water and grease drip out before you put the measure into the hot dog. (If you don't properly drain the chili, it will make the assembled hot dog too soggy.) Sprinkle with finely chopped onion, if wanted, along with other go-withs, if wanted.

If you want a chili dog, leave out the wiener and add a double serving of chili, very well drained.

One secret of Ed's chili was that he kept a pot bubbling hot (but not boiling) all day and on into the night, adding a new batch to it as needed. The chili was quite thin, containing quite a bit of accumulated grease, making the draining part even more important.

Anyhow, try the recipe above, adding to it as you see fit. Make it thin and greasy and let it simmer until needed. When you get the recipe down pat, double or triple it for serving a crowd.

Bus Station Chili

Sylvia's Family Soul Food Cookbook, written by Sylvia Woods, who owns a famous restaurant in Harlem, sets forth an interesting chili recipe from Hemingway, South Carolina. The recipe is from an old restaurant, the A&J, that was located in the bus station, and was submitted to the Soul Food *book by Camellia Chinned Lane, the daughter of one of the owners of the restaurant. The chili was served in bowls; in sloppy joes; and as a*

CHILI

topper for hot dogs, hamburgers, and hamburger steaks. The recipe can be increased as needed.

  1 pound ground beef
  1 cup chopped onion
  1½ cups tomato sauce
  ½ cup water
  2 tablespoons chili powder
  ½ teaspoon salt
  ½ teaspoon pepper

Brown the meat and onion in a large skillet. Drain off the fat. Stir in the chili powder, salt, and black pepper. Add the tomato sauce and water. Bring to a boil, reduce the heat, and simmer for 10 to 15 minutes or until thickened. Serve hot or warm as a chili, or use as a filling or topper.

Chili Dip

This dip works best with chili made from finely ground meat. Market-grind beef will be satisfactory.

  2 cups precooked chili
  ½ cup grated cheddar
  ¼ cup minced onion
  1 tablespoon minced chives

Heat all the ingredients in a saucepan, stirring as you go with a wooden spoon. Use as a dip with crackers or Fritos. This makes a good way to use up a small amount of leftovers.

178

Chili Meat Loaf

Anyone who loves the taste of chili will like this recipe. It works best with ground beef chuck. If it is made with very lean meat, such as venison or ostrich, add a little beef fat (suet) or bacon drippings. Seasoned with chili powder mix, the loaf is also served with a commercial chili sauce (tomato based).

1½ pound ground meat
½ cup finely chopped onion
½ cup finely chopped red bell pepper
2 seeded and finely chopped jalapeño peppers
2 finely chopped cloves garlic
2 chicken eggs
beef bouillon cube dissolved in hot water
3 tablespoons melted butter
3 tablespoons bread crumbs
2 tablespoons chili powder
salt and freshly ground black pepper to taste
chili sauce

Preheat the oven to 350°F and grease a Pyrex meat loaf pan. In a large bowl, mix all the ingredients except the melted butter, bread crumbs, and chili sauce. Turn out into the meat loaf pan. Sprinkle with bread crumbs, brush with melted butter, and place in the center of the oven for 1 hour. Turn off the heat and let the loaf coast in the hot oven for 15 minutes. Serve in slices, topped with warmed chili sauce.

Chili Casserole

I've seen dozens of casserole-type recipes that call for chili. Often these recipes come from community or fund-raiser cookbooks, in which the contributors, usually women, use canned or packaged ingredients instead of fresh or freshly made. Leftover chili can be used instead of canned, if available, and fried tortilla strips can be substituted for the corn chips.

3 (14-ounce) cans chile con carne or about 4 cups leftover chili
1 large bag corn chips
4 chopped onions, medium to large
1 pound grated yellow cheese

Preheat the oven to 300°F and grease a large casserole dish. Line the dish with one-third of the bag of corn chips. Spread on 1 can of chili. (If using homemade chili, substitute 1½ cups for each can.) Sprinkle on a layer of onions and cheese, using about a third of each. Repeat the layers until the ingredients are used up. Cover the dish with aluminum foil. Bake in the center of the oven for 1½ hours. If necessary, broil a few minutes with the foil removed to lightly brown the top layer. Serve hot, possibly with noodles, corn on the cob, hot bread, and so on.

Note: Other casserole dishes, some called Texas Hash, make use of ground beef, chile peppers of one sort or another, and chili powder.

Chili Tacos

This recipe works best with chili made from finely ground meat, but small chunks of meat can also be used if they are very tender. In either case, a rather basic chili—without beans and extenders—should be used.

Make your own tortillas or use those found in refrigerated sections of the supermarket. Prepared taco shells can also be used, but these are often too hard and brittle for easy eating. If you make your own from fresh tortillas, you can fry them until lightly brown but still limp. Note that in this recipe the main stuffing is put into a tortilla, which is then folded and deep-fried. Various toppings are added at the table. I must point out that most taco recipes call for hard shells, preshaped and prefried—crunchy and sometimes difficult to eat without spilling stuff out. Suit yourself.

  12 (8-inch) corn tortillas
  2 cups cooked no-bean chili
  1 (8-ounce) can tomato sauce
  1 medium-to-large onion, minced
  ½ medium-sized green bell pepper, seeded and minced
  ½ medium-sized red bell pepper, seeded and minced
  1 head lettuce, shredded
  2 medium-to-large tomatoes, finely chopped
  bowl of grated sharp cheddar cheese
  bowl of chunky tomato-based salsa
  salt and freshly ground pepper to taste
  peanut oil for deep-frying

Rig for deep-frying, heating 3 or 4 inches of peanut oil in a suitable pot to about 350°F. While waiting, heat the chili in a skillet, adding the onion and peppers. Cook for at least 5 minutes, stirring a time or two with a wooden spoon, and then stir in the tomato sauce, salt, and pepper. Simmer and stir until the oil in the pot is hot enough to deep-fry. Place a soft tortilla on a work surface and add about one-twelfth of the chili mixture in the middle, leaving plenty of room for the toppings. Fold the semi-filled tortilla, hold it by the ends with tongs, and dip it into the hot oil until it is golden and firm, but not hard. Drain and repeat until all the tacos have been partly filled and fried. Serve hot, along with bowls of shredded lettuce, chopped tomatoes, salsa, and grated cheese. Other toppings, such as sour cream, guacamole, Tabasco, and so on, can be offered if desired.

Tex-Mex Pizzas

Thick leftover chili can be used as a meat topping for pizzas. I usually prefer to make the following recipe using 8-inch flour tortillas for the crust. These are very easy to make, and they come in handy for a light lunch, if you don't object to the rather thin crust. Any good chili will work, but I really prefer a recipe with lots of meat and no beans. Finely chopped mushrooms, onions, and so on can be added, but I find that a chunky tomato-based salsa contains what I want—and it's readily available in any supermarket in mild, medium, or hot.

    leftover chili
    8-inch flour tortillas
    chunky salsa (mild, medium, or hot)
    shredded jack cheese
    salt and black pepper to taste

Preheat the broiler and rig the top of the baking sheet about 4 inches from the heat. Spread the leftover chili over the tortilla, then spread on a layer of salsa. Sprinkle lightly with salt and pepper. Sprinkle on a topping of shredded cheese. Broil for a few minutes under high heat, or until the top of the cheese browns and starts to blister here and there. Eat hot with Mexican beer.

Chili Joes

Here's an easy dish that I like to make with leftover chili, preferably without beans.

leftover chili
buns
shredded cheese
chopped scallions, including part of green tops

Heat the chili in a skillet. If it is thin, simmer uncovered until part of the liquid cooks off. Open the buns and lightly toast each half under a broiler. Put the buns two up on a plate. Top generously with chili. Sprinkle with cheese and a few minced scallions. Eat with a fork. A tossed salad goes nicely on the side.

18

CHILI GO-WITHS

At this stage of the game, after all I've been through, I shouldn't be surprised at anything related to chili recipes and menus. But I am, constantly. Still, chili has come a long way in recent years and deserves more than soda crackers and beer. Here are a few topics that fit in with a bowl of red. A few major ingredients, such as beans, have been discussed in previous chapters as well as in the text below simply because they can be used as an ingredient cooked in the chili or as a go-with or topping.

CHEESE AND DAIRY PRODUCTS

Some dairy products fit right in with chili because of the taste and because milk is one of the few things that will help tame the bite of capsaicin. But there are limits.

Sour Cream and Yogurt. I was a little shocked when I, a country boy, first encountered sour cream in a bowl of red. But it turns out to be one of the better modern additions to chili. It is best when served as a topping—1 or 2 tablespoons per bowl of red—for rather thick chili. It works especially well with very hot (spicy) chili.

Plain yogurt can be used in chili instead of sour cream. Also try yogurt cheese, which is easily made at home by straining the whey from plain yogurt. I use a coffee filter fitted into the drip cup of a discarded coffeemaker, letting the yogurt drain 10 or 12 hours. Good stuff. I also use the yogurt cheese for some recipes calling for cream cheese, which is not unheard of in chili—Philly Chili, of course.

Some recipes call for several sorts of dairy products. A Maryland chilihead, for example, specifies 2 cups plain yogurt, ½ cup light cream, and ½ cup sour cream for the pot, and another pint of sour cream for the toppings.

Although I have reluctantly come to be a staunch champion of sour cream as a topping in chili, and, later, of yogurt, and even old-time clabber, I'll have to draw a line, insisting on the plain stuff made from whole cow's milk or goat's milk. There are limits beyond which we should not venture if we want to retain the unprissified mystique of chili. Crème fraîche, as recommended by a large New York hunting and fishing magazine, is going too far.

Cheese. Cheese is sometimes put into chili during the cooking phase, but it is more often used as a topping. Some recipes recommend one kind of cheese as an ingredient, cooked in the pot, and another kind as an optional topping. For either purpose, a firm cheddar is hard to beat and is available in several tastes, from mild to sharp. Any of the jack cheeses, such as Monterey Jack, are good but are a little too soft to suit me as a topping. Aged jack is much better, if you can find it. If you read many chili recipes, you'll likely find all manner of cheeses, such as Havarti, used as an ingredient or topping.

While working on this book, I ordered a bowl of chili for lunch in my favorite local greasy spoon. The chili was good if not anything special—but it was served with a delicious toasted cheese sandwich, made pretty much as follows.

Toasted Cheese Sandwiches

These are excellent and quite filling when served with a hot bowl of chili. The combination makes an excellent lunch for a hungry person on a cold day.

ordinary white bread
cheddar cheese
butter

Melt the butter in a skillet. Sandwich some cheese, preferably several thin slices or sprinkles of shredded cheese, between two pieces of ordinary white bread. Put the sandwich into the skillet and weight it with a bacon press. Cook for 2 minutes, or until the bottom is lightly browned. Turn, press, and cook for another 2 minutes or so. Cut the sandwich in half diagonally and serve hot.

Variations: I often brush both sides of the sandwich with butter and grill it for 3 minutes in a George Foreman grill. As a variation, try an open-faced cheese sandwich, cooked under a broiler until the cheese browns and starts to blister.

BEANS

Although beans are commonly used as an ingredient added to the pot of chili during the cooking phase, as discussed in chapter 5, I think it is best to cook them separately and serve them as a side dish. That way, partakers can eat them along with the chili, or perhaps dump them into the bowl if they feel so inclined.

Most kinds of dry beans require long cooking or long soaking, but others don't. Although some of the gourmet beans such as calypso and Jacob's cattle are very attractive and tasty, I usually cook ordinary dry pinto beans, more or less following the recipe below. If you have a better recipe, or a better chili bean, use it.

A. D.'s Pinto Beans

Most cookbooks advise us to soak pinto beans (and most others) overnight or several hours before cooking them. The soaking allows them to be cooked for a shorter period of time, but it does not reduce the flatulence, as has been reported. I prefer to cook them for a long time without presoaking, especially if I am cooking a pot of chili at the same time. How long should they be cooked? Until they are done but not mushy. Almost al dente—but not quite. The exact times seem to vary with each batch of beans. I have written several recipes for pinto beans, all following the basic procedure set forth here. One of my variations included a couple of wild bird peppers, dried reds. These imparted a haunting flavor to the bean. If such a pepper isn't readily available to you, try a dried cayenne or your favorite red pepper flakes from the spice rack. Some mail-order outfits provide dozens of kinds of red pepper flakes, and a few offer dried bird peppers.

> 1 (16-ounce) package dry pinto beans
> 1 ham bone with a little meat on it
> 1 medium-to-large onion, chopped
> wild bird peppers or red pepper flakes
> salt to taste
> water

Dump the beans into a pan of water and discard any that float. Drain the beans and put them into a pot with the ham bone. Cover with hot water. Crumble the bird peppers into the pot, using seeds and all. Bring to a boil and add the chopped onion and salt. Reduce the heat to low, cover tightly, and simmer for a couple of hours, until the meat is falling off the ham bone and the beans are done to your liking. While the beans simmer, stir from time to time and add some hot water as needed, remembering that the beans will soak up lots of water as they cook and expand. Serve the cooked beans on the side with a bowl of chili, or, if you must, stir some into the chili shortly before eating. Consider a chunk or two of meat from the ham bone as a bonus for the cook.

Note: These beans can be refrigerated, or frozen, but they are at their best when freshly cooked, especially if you appreciate a crunchy bean.

Refried Beans and Frijoles Con Queso

Refried beans go nicely with chili. They can be stirred into the chili as a thickener, or served separately. I like to put a chunky, thick chili on one side of a plate and the refried beans on the other, getting a little of both in each bit. Start with some fully cooked pinto beans. Canned will do. Heat some bacon drippings or lard in a heavy skillet. Add a few of the cooked beans, mash, and stir in a little water. Repeat until all the beans are gone, or until you have all the refries you want. Salt to taste and continue cooking until the mass is thick enough to serve on a plate.

For Frijoles con Queso, add a little minced jalapeño to the bacon drippings, cook as directed above, and add some coarsely shredded Monterey Jack cheese at the end, stirring just long enough to melt the cheese. Serve on the side with chili and rolled tortillas.

CORN AND CORN PRODUCTS

In addition to its use as a thickener for chili (chapter 6), cornmeal is also used in making tortillas and corn pone. Also, corn chips are often used as a go-with or topping for chili. Some prefer yellow corn chips; others, white.

Hominy makes a good chili go-with. Both white and yellow canned hominy are available at most large supermarkets. Dried hominy, sometimes called posole, can be found at some southwestern and specialized markets. It is available in white, yellow, blue, and red. Whatever the color, it is quite hard, so soak it for several hours and cook until it is soft. Note that dried hominy will expand like beans or rice, so start with about half the amount you want to end up with and be sure to keep plenty of liquid in the pot.

Hominy and grits are often confused by those not familiar with them. They are different corn products, and the term "hominy grits" is misleading. Grits aren't normally served with chili. I wouldn't be surprised, however, to see a recipe calling for polenta on the side, as Italian grits are called.

And of course you can't beat a side of cornbread, in any form, as a go-with for your favorite chili.

RICE AND PASTA

Some chili recipes, especially from Cincinnati and other hot spots in the Midwest, call for spaghetti, noodles, and other kinds of pasta to be cooked in the chili or to be served with it. Some of these recipes were covered in chapter 16. If the pasta is to be served on the side, or used as a bed for chili, cook it according to the directions on the package, or by your favorite recipe if you make your own pasta from scratch.

Rice is also used in chili as an ingredient, as discussed in chapter 5, but I really prefer to cook it separately and use it as a topping in a bowl of chili—a white dollop centered in the bowl of red. I also use rice as a bed when serving chili in a plate. In any case, ordinary long-grain rice will do.

Two-Day Chili Over Rice

While some chili and recipes work better when the rice is added to the bowl last, this one is the other way around, owing partly to a dollop of sour cream added to each bowl shortly before serving.

3 pounds beef chuck, cut into 1-inch cubes
3 cups beef broth
3 cups cooked long-grain rice (fluffy)
1 (16-ounce) can pinto beans
¼ cup chili powder
2 tablespoons cooking oil
2 tablespoons flour
1 tablespoon fresh oregano, chopped
4 cloves garlic, chopped
1 jalapeño, seeded and minced
2 teaspoons freshly ground cumin
salt and pepper to taste
sour cream
lime wedges

Heat the oil in a stovetop Dutch oven or other suitable pot. Brown the beef, stirring as you go with a wooden spoon. Stir in the garlic and jalapeño. Reduce the heat to low, then stir in the flour, chili powder, cumin, and oregano. Add the beef broth, salt, and pepper.

Bring to a light boil. Reduce the heat, cover tightly, and simmer for 2 hours, stirring from time to time and adding a little water if needed. Cool on the stovetop and then put the whole pot into the refrigerator overnight. Shortly before eating time, remove the pot and flake off any fat that has hardened on the surface. Heat the pot until the chili is hot. Stir in the beans and cook for a few minutes. Spoon about ½ cup of rice into each serving bowl. Then spoon in the chili, but do not stir. Top each bowl with about 1 tablespoon of sour cream. Serve with a lime wedge on the side, in case anyone wants to kick it up with a little juice. I also like to have a bottle of Tabasco at hand. Feeds 6 to 10.

A. D.'s Bird Pepper Rice

Several kinds of wild peppers can be used in this recipe, including the tepin and the chiletepin.

2 cups long-grain rice
1–2 dried bird peppers
butter
salt to taste
4 cups water

Lightly butter the bottom and sides of a suitable pot. Bring the water to a boil. Crumble the peppers over the pot, letting seeds and all fall in. Sprinkle in a little salt and add the rice. Bring the water to a new boil, reduce the heat to a simmer, cover tightly, and cook for 20 minutes. Do not peek. Remove the cover and fluff up the rice with a fork before serving.

Dumplings

Dumplings are not standard additions to chili, but they really hit the spot on a cold night. Cornmeal dumplings are especially good in chili if successfully made, and can work as a tightener as well as an extender. See my corndodger recipe in chapter 14. Also note that easy dumplings can be made from strips of fresh flour or corn tortillas, or perhaps from pieces of wide-band noodles or pasta.

Almost always, ordinary flour dumplings are added during the last 20 minutes or so of cooking. Try your favorite dumpling recipe, or adapt one from a family cookbook. Many dumplings are rolled out like pizza dough and cut into strips. I like spoon dumplings, as made from the following quick-mix recipe.

Chili with Bisquick Dumplings

It's best to use dumplings with a thin chili cooked or reheated in a Dutch oven or other widemouthed pot. The wider the pot, the more dumplings it will float.

> pot of chili with a thin gravy
> 2 cups Bisquick
> ⅔ cup milk

Mix the Bisquick and milk. Wet a small spoon and drop the mix a spoonful at a time into the simmering pot of chili. Continue until all the mix has been used, or until the surface is crowded with floating dumplings. Do not overcrowd. Simmer uncovered about 10 minutes. Serve hot in bowls, allowing each partaker 2 or 3 dumplings.

CRACKERS AND BREADS

Most people will want some sort of bread with their chili, either to be eaten out of hand or crumbled into the bowl. The latter method is useful when the chili is steaming hot or has a little too much grease floating on top. Rolled tortillas are also used for sopping. Here are the favorites:

Saltines. Often called soda crackers, saltines make a popular go-with for chili. Some chili parlors and truck stops advertise all the crackers you can eat with a bowl of red. Many people eat a cracker along with each spoon of chili, especially if the chili is on the thick side or if it is quite spicy. If the chili is thin, many of us will crumble the crackers into the bowl, and I confess to a fondness for this method. Thus, the cracker acts as a filler or extender—and serves to soak up some of the grease off the top, making it less obvious and easier to swallow.

Any good soda cracker will do, and the compleat chilihead can make his own at home. I do, however, avoid the newfangled reduced-sodium kinds on the grounds that a saltine cracker must contain some salt. If your saltines happen to be stale or don't have the characteristic crunch, fit them onto a broiling sheet, brush with melted butter, and broil close to the heat for a minute or two. If done correctly, these are so good that you may want to toast them whether they are stale or not. But be warned that crackers burn easily, so watch them closely.

Oyster Crackers. These float nicely and look good in a bowl of red and, reportedly, they were invented in a chili parlor in the Midwest. The eatery in question also sold oysters, which may explain the name. Maybe their main use was as a topping to oyster stew. In any case, they float better than most crackers, but they don't crumble as nicely.

Tortillas. These are the classic go-with for chili. Both corn and flour tortillas can be used, and are readily available these days from ordinary supermarkets, usually refrigerated and ready for warming. For chili, the cornmeal kind is best, I think. And these are even better if you make your own from freshly ground cornmeal instead of from the dry and usually tasteless masa harina marketed in packages.

In either case, it's best to serve the tortillas moist and warm so that they can be rolled and eaten out of one hand while the other wields the spoon. Tortillas can also be cut into little triangular strips and fried, making a chip that goes nicely with chili. These can be eaten out of hand, or crumbled into the chili like crackers. Also, the whole strips (not fried) can be added to the chili like dumplings.

To make your own tortillas, mix the finely ground cornmeal with enough lard to form a paste. Place a tablespoonful into a tortilla press. Pull the handle and you have a perfectly flat round. (You can also pat them out by hand, if you have skill enough.) Sticking can be a problem, sometimes solved by mashing the dough between sheets of wax paper. Have a hot skillet or griddle ready and cook each tortilla a minute on each side, until done but not crisp. A good deal depends on the thickness and consistency of your cornmeal, but in a few minutes you'll be turning out almost perfect tortillas.

Lady Bird Johnson's Noche Specials

Here's an excellent chili go-with from Lady Bird Johnson. It's best when made with fresh tortillas, but refrigerated or frozen store-bought rounds will do. Any good grated cheese will work. Try grated cheddar or perhaps Monterey Jack.

corn tortillas, about 5 inches in diameter
cooking oil for deep-frying
grated cheese
fresh jalapeño peppers

Preheat the oven to 350°F and rig for deep-frying. While waiting, cut the peppers in half lengthwise and carefully remove the seeds and inner pith along with the stem. Cut the tortillas into quarters, pie shaped. Fry these in hot fat until nicely browned and crisp on each side. Drain the chips and place a slice of jalapeño on each piece. Top with 1 heaping teaspoon of grated cheese. Place in a baking sheet and cook in the center of the oven until the cheese melts. Serve hot along with chili.

Corn Bread and Corndodgers. Don't worry. I'm not going to get started here on the right stuff for making good corn bread. Any kind of corn bread can be used with chili. I'll take hoecake, made without soda or other leavening. Some people crumble corn bread into chili; some chili parlors even encourage the practice in their advertising, and a few even serve the chili over crumbled corn bread.

Corn bread sticks, by the way, are very good with chili and are easy to hold and eat.

A. D.'s Jalapeño Bread

Here's a favorite of mine for eating with chili and other meat stews. A green jalapeño will certainly work, but a red one is better, if available.

2 cups fine stone-ground white cornmeal
2½ cups hot water, more or less
1½ tablespoons peanut oil, plus a little more
1 jalapeño
1 teaspoon salt

Preheat the oven to 400°F. Put a little of the peanut oil into a 10½-inch cast-iron skillet, coating the bottom and sides. Mix the cornmeal, 1½ tablespoons of oil, and salt in a bowl. Stir in most of the water, slowly adding more and a little more until you have a nice mush. Let it sit while you remove the seeds and inner membranes from the jalapeño. Cut the jalapeño in half lengthwise, quarter, then mince the strips. Stir the pepper into the cornmeal mush, adding more water if needed. Put the mixture into the skillet, smooth out, and place in the center of the oven for 30 or 40 minutes, or until the corn bread has a crispy crust on the sides and top. During the last 10 minutes of cooking, brush the top with a little oil. If the top is slow to brown, finish it off under the broiler. When hot, this bread will have a crisp surface and a soft, moist inside, which is the way I like it. Cooks and writers who say that corn bread is dry don't understand the real stuff.

Variation: Increase the amount of fresh pepper, maybe adding a little red and green. If you want the bread really hot, leave the seeds, or part of them, in the jalapeño.

Sourdough. I don't normally serve any sort of rolls, biscuits, or loaf bread with chili, partly because the traditional crackers and corn tortillas work so well. I would, however, like to pass on a tip from Big Bruce Pinnell, Chief Executive Pepper for Gunpowder Foods, Inc. Scoop the center out of a large sourdough roll and use it as an edible bowl for the chili. I have seen this served from a booth at a chili cook-off.

SALADS AND RAW VEGETABLES

Raw vegetables are sometimes served with chili as optional go-withs or toppings; these include cauliflower florets, carrot sticks, and so on. Raw tomatoes are especially popular, either sliced or chopped. Sliced Vidalia onions are also good on the side, along with chopped onions to be used as a topping. Fresh scallions, chilled in ice and served from a glass or tall bowl, are also nice.

Somehow, chef's salads, Waldorfs, and other such productions just don't fit in with chili. Instead of a salad, I prefer a small bowl of chunky tomato-based salsa on the side. But suit yourself.

Small pickled peppers are served with chili, and sometimes they are floated in the bowl. Some sports put a few hot chili-piquins into the chili, hoping that somebody will dare to bite into one. Jalapeño peppers are sometimes cut into sticks and served on the side. These are called Texas toothpicks.

DRINKS

Beer is hard to beat for most Texans and bibulous adults. Cold hard cider also works with chili, albeit far from traditional. Forget the wine. If you want something stronger than beer, try a tequila fizz made with freshly squeezed lime juice, or perhaps a bloody Maria. The tomato juice in the latter seems to help, and I confess to sometimes drinking an old hangover remedy called redeye, made by mixing ice-cold beer and ice-cold tomato juice in a 12-ounce glass, along with a squirt or two of Worcestershire and, for chili, a drop or two of Tabasco.

It's iced tea or cola for teetotalers and children. Cool springwater will do. If the chili is very hot, however, even iced water won't help much. It's best to serve buttermilk or some dairy product such as sour cream, yogurt, or clabber, all of which help cut the capsaicin. People from the Caucasus may prefer chilled kefir, an alcoholic beverage made from fermented camel's milk—and Mongols will surely insist on kumiss, made from fermented mare's milk, pointing out that it is a digestive aid and therefore perfect for chili. Maybe it is—but I don't care. I'll have to draw the line somewhere.

METRIC CONVERSION TABLES

Metric U.S. Approximate Equivalents

Liquid Ingredients

Metric	U.S. Measures	Metric	U.S. Measures
1.23 ML	¼ TSP.	29.57 ML	2 TBSP.
2.36 ML	½ TSP.	44.36 ML	3 TBSP.
3.70 ML	¾ TSP.	59.15 ML	¼ CUP
4.93 ML	1 TSP.	118.30 ML	½ CUP
6.16 ML	1¼ TSP.	236.59 ML	1 CUP
7.39 ML	1½ TSP.	473.18 ML	2 CUPS OR 1 PT.
8.63 ML	1¾ TSP.	709.77 ML	3 CUPS
9.86 ML	2 TSP.	946.36 ML	4 CUPS OR 1 QT.
14.79 ML	1 TBSP.	3.79 L	4 QTS. OR 1 GAL.

Dry Ingredients

Metric	U.S. Measures	Metric		U.S. Measures
2 (1.8) G	⅟₁₆ OZ.	80 G		2⅘ OZ.
3½ (3.5) G	⅛ OZ.	85 (84.9) G		3 OZ.
7 (7.1) G	¼ OZ.	100 G		3½ OZ.
15 (14.2) G	½ OZ.	115 (113.2) G		4 OZ.
21 (21.3) G	¾ OZ.	125 G		4½ OZ.
25 G	⅞ OZ.	150 G		5¼ OZ.
30 (28.3) G	1 OZ.	250 G		8⅞ OZ.
50 G	1¾ OZ.	454 G	1 LB.	16 OZ.
60 (56.6) G	2 OZ.	500 G	1 LIVRE	17⅗ OZ.

Acknowledgments

A few of the recipes used in this book were adapted from the author's cooking column in *Gray's Sporting Journal*. Acknowledgments to other authors and books are made in the text as appropriate. I also thank Alaska Northwest Books for permission to quote a recipe by Ed Martley from the book *Cooking Alaskan*.

Index

sauces and condiments,
79–80
Scotch as a thinner, 63
Scoville scale, 10
secret ingredients, 146
seeds and nuts, 64
Senator's Chili, 36–37
Senator's Chili Mix, 37
serving chili, 28
sesame seed oil, 67
shark, 123–24
Shelby, Carroll, 35–36
simmering, 27
Six Gun Chili, 39–40
skillets, 24–25
Slinger, 175
Smith, H. Allen, 138–39,
160, 166
soda pop as a thinner, 62
sour cream, 184, 185
sourdough bread, 197
sours, 82
soybeans, 52
spice mixes, 78–79
spices and herbs, 74–79
spoon coatings, 64–68
squirrel, 123–24
Stevens, Jackie, 28
stoves and outdoor cooking
rigs, 23
suet and tallow, 66
sugar, 80–81
Super Slinger, 175

supermarket chili, spices, and
powders, 161–62
*Swamp Cookin' with the River
People* (Holyfield), 106
Swampman Dan's Deer Meat
Chili, 106
sweets, 80–81
*Sylvia's Family Soul Food
Cookbook* (Woods), 177–78

Tabasco sauce, 79, 173
Tampa Bay Three-Bean Chili,
49–51
Taos Old-Time Roast Pork
Green Chili, 87–89
Tenderfoot Chili (family
style), 39
tequila as a thinner, 62
Terlingua, TX, 35, 138, 151,
166, 167
Tex-Mex Pizzas, 182
Texas chili, 154–56
thickeners and tighteners,
63–64
thinners, 60–63
Three-Way Chili, 40–41
Toasted Cheese Sandwiches, 186
tomatoes and tomato products,
70–71
tortillas, 181, 194–95
Tower, Senator John, 36, 37
Trinity of Cajun or Creole
cooking, 55

Enjoy more wit and wisdom from A.D. Livingston
with these titles from Lyons Press,
available from your favorite bookseller

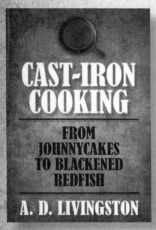

CAST-IRON COOKING
FROM JOHNNYCAKES TO BLACKENED REDFISH
A. D. LIVINGSTON

COLD-SMOKING & SALT-CURING
MEAT, FISH, & GAME
A. D. LIVINGSTON

JERKY
MAKE YOUR OWN DELICIOUS JERKY AND JERKY DISHES USING BEEF, VENISON, FISH, OR FOWL
A. D. LIVINGSTON

SAUSAGE
OVER 100 DELICIOUS RECIPES FOR SAUSAGES AND SAUSAGE DISHES
A. D. LIVINGSTON

CHILI
RECIPES FOR A BODACIOUS BOWL OF RED
A. D. LIVINGSTON

THE CURMUDGEON'S BOOK OF SKILLET COOKING
MORE THAN 101 EASY RECIPES FOR JACKLEG COOKS, ONE-ARMED CHEFS, AND PRACTICAL HOUSEWIVES
A. D. LIVINGSTON

LyonsPress.com

About the Author

A. D. Livingston claims to have hop-scotched through life. Navy at seventeen. Mechanical engineering at Auburn. Atomic bombs at Oak Ridge. Creative writing at University of Alabama. Missiles and rockets at Huntsville. Published a novel and played a little poker. Travel editor at *Southern Living* magazine. Freelance writing and outdoor photography. Word man for fishing rods and bait-casting reels with Lew Childre, the genius of modern fishing tackle. Bought the family farm. Lost the back forty publishing *Bass Fishing News*. Lost the rest of the farm manufacturing fishing lures. Back to freelancing. Published twenty-something books. Food columnist for *Gray's Sporting Journal*. He hates to work, but all his life he has loved to hunt and fish and to cook and eat the bounty. And he loves to write about it his way.